How to Run a

How to Run a Charity

Second edition

Cecile Gillard

The Governance
Institute

First published 2013
This edition published 2017

Published by ICSA Publishing Limited
Saffron House
6–10 Kirby Street
London EC1N 8TS
© ICSA Publishing Limited, 2017

Typeset by Paul Barrett Book Production, Cambridge
Printed in Great Britain by Lightning Source, Milton Keynes, Buckinghamshire

British Cataloguing in Publication Data
A catalogue record for this book is available from the British Library.

ISBN 9781860726965

Contents

CONTENTS

Table of statutes

Note: care should be taken to ensure any copy of legislation being consulted contains all amendments currently in force: see www.legislation.gov.uk.

England and Wales – charity law

Charities Act 2011 as amended by the Charities (Protection and Social Investment) Act 2016

Accounts:	The Charities (Accounts and Reports) Regulations 2008
CIOs:	The Charitable Incorporated Organisations (General) Regulations 2012 The Charitable Incorporated Organisations (Insolvency and Dissolution) Regulations 2012
Disposals of land:	The Charities (Qualified Surveyors' Reports) Regulations 1992
Fundraising (street and house-to-house collections):	House to House Collections Act 1939 Police, Factories & c. (Miscellaneous Provisions) Act 1916

Scotland – charity law

Charities and Trustee Investment (Scotland) Act 2005 (as amended by the Public Services Reform (Scotland) Act 2010)

Fundraising:	The Charities and Benevolent Fundraising (Scotland) Regulations 2009
Reorganisation:	The Charities Reorganisation (Scotland) Regulations 2007 The Charities Reorganisation (Scotland) Amendment Regulations 2012 The Charities Restricted Funds Reorganisation (Scotland) Regulations 2012

Accounts:	The Charities Accounts (Scotland) Regulations 2006 The Charities Accounts (Scotland) Amendment Regulations 2010 The Charities Accounts (Scotland) Amendment (No.2) Regulations 2014 The Charities Accounts (Scotland) Amendment Regulations 2016
Disclosures (documents, etc):	The Charities References in Documents (Scotland) Regulations 2007 The Charities References in Documents (Scotland) Amendment Regulations 2008
SCIOs:	The Scottish Charitable Incorporated Organisations Regulations 2011 The Scottish Charitable Incorporated Organisations (Removal from the Register and Dissolution) Regulations 2011

Northern Ireland – charity law

Charities Act (Northern Ireland) 2008 and various supplementary statutory instruments

UK – company law

Companies Act 2006
Plus numerous statutory instruments (i.e. various regulations made to supplement the Companies Act)

Other

Bribery Act 2010
Data Protection Act 1998
Equality Act 2010
Gambling Act 2005
Health and Safety at Work Act 1974
Health and Safety (Offences) Act 2008
Protection of Freedoms Act 2012
Safeguarding of Vulnerable Groups Act 2006

Acronyms and abbreviations

AGM	annual general meeting
CASC	community amateur sports club
CIC	community interest company
CIO	charitable incorporated organisation
DBS	Disclosure and Barring Service
HMRC	Her Majesty's Revenue & Customs
IHT	Inheritance Tax
IoF	Institute of Fundraising
The OSCR	The Office of the Scottish Charity Regulator
PAYE	Pay As You Earn
PSC	persons with significant control
RODRA	Register of Directors' Residential Addresses
SAIL	single alternative inspection location
SCIO	Scottish charitable incorporated organisation
SORP	Statement of Recommended Practice – Accounting by Charities
TUPE Regulations	Transfer of Undertakings (Protection of Employment) Regulations

Preface

This book addresses the practical legal administration of charities, against the background of the charity regulatory regimes of the UK and the charity law applicable in each of the UK's individual jurisdictions. It is primarily aimed at those who have principal responsibility for the governance, administration and practical operation of charities, in particular their trustees and secretaries or clerks and senior charity managers, and those who support and advise them, including lawyers, accountants, chartered secretaries and other professional advisers. There have been significant recent changes in law and regulation, governance standards and regulatory practice and expectations which are addressed in this new edition.

Charities are part of the voluntary or civil society sector. They are sometimes, rather misleadingly, described as 'not-for-profit' organisations. In fact they can and should generate a surplus on their activities in order to make themselves financially sustainable. What distinguishes charities from commercial organisations in relation to profits (i.e. surpluses) is how they use those surplus funds – applying them to activities in pursuit of their charitable purposes that provide charitable public benefits.

Charities, above any other organisations, are outward facing, operating for the benefit of people who are not inherently part of the charity itself. Every charity provides benefits to the wider public, even if it has a specific beneficiary group as its prime focus. Charity trustees are usually unpaid volunteers, and charity members have no commercial ownership of the charity and gain no significant financial or other material benefits from their membership.

Charities are wonderfully diverse in size, structure and activities. They can take many different legal forms, although three particular forms have always been most commonly used – unincorporated trusts, unincorporated members' associations and charitable companies limited by guarantee. Since these three forms are far more common than any of the alternatives, this book particularly highlights the law and regulations specific to each of them, as well as setting out the principles common to all charities.

The introduction of charitable incorporated organisations (CIOs) and Scottish charitable incorporated organisations (SCIOs) offers a new optional corporate body legal form specifically for charities. Where there are significant rules applicable to CIOs or SCIOs or different require-ments or obligations for them, this is indicated.

CIOs and SCIOs should be distinguished from community interest companies (CICs). These are a special type of limited company, primarily intended for social enterprise and community benefit activities. CICs are not permitted to be charities. CICs must meet the 'community interest test' which is specific to CICs (it does not apply to charities).

Certain fundamental principles remain of general application to all charities across the UK. However, there is specific statutory-based charity law for each of the jurisdictions – England and Wales, Scotland and Northern Ireland. Each of these jurisdictions also has its own charity registration and regulatory regime. This book therefore points out some key legal or regulatory requirements that are specific to each of those jurisdictions.

The book uses the following terms:

- Charitable company – a company registered under company law that is a charity (usually such a company is limited by guarantee).
- Incorporated charity – a charity that has incorporated legal form (e.g. a charitable company, a CIO or a SCIO). Incorporated charities provide limited liability protection for their members and their trustees.
- Unincorporated charity – a charity that does not have incorporated form (e.g. a trust or an unincorporated members' association). Unincorporated charities do not have their own legal identity or independent legal capacity and do not provide limited liability protection for their trustees (or their members, if they have a membership structure).

For charities in England and Wales, the most substantial legal and regulatory obligations are placed on *registered* charities, so in relation to that jurisdiction this book concentrates on the regulatory regime for registered charities. The position is different in Scotland, as all charities are registered on the Scottish Charity Register, so the only variations in charity regulation in Scotland are the 'lighter touch' requirements for smaller charities on the Register (for example, in accounting and reporting requirements).

It is a privilege and a pleasure to serve the charity sector across the UK. I never cease to be amazed at the good that charities do and the positive impact they have on society, especially with such limited resources. Well done and please keep up this wonderful work!

Cecile Gillard
June 2017

1   Legal and regulatory context

What a charity is in law: the key legal factors that make an organisation a charity

Being a charity is a legal status, attained by meeting the applicable legal conditions. It is a status that is potentially open to many – but not all – different types of organisation. For example, community interest companies cannot be used for charitable purposes. This special legal status must be justified – it is a legal privilege rather than a legal right.

The legal test of what a 'charity' is for charity law and charity regulatory purposes should not be confused with:

- the individual organisation's *legal form* (i.e. what kind of legal organisation it is); or
- other legal tests relevant to charities, such as the tax law test that must be met for an organisation to seek charity tax relief and tax exemptions.

Under the law of England and Wales, the legal conditions that must be met, in order to be a charity, are:

- the organisation has exclusively charitable purposes (these fall within the 'descriptions' of potentially charitable purposes set out in the Charities Act 2011); and
- that the organisation's specific purposes are 'for the public benefit'.

If these conditions are met, the organisation is, in law, a charity. Significant consequences flow from that legal status, particularly in relation to the provision of public benefit, the protection and proper use of the charity's funds and assets, the duties and responsibilities of its charity trustees, the regulation of the organisation and its public accountability.

A charity's charitable purposes are normally specified in its constitution (which is sometimes described as its governing instrument or governing document). They are specific to that charity and it must pursue those purposes but not go beyond them.

The legal test of what is a charity in Scotland is known as 'the charity test' (see section 7 of the Charities and Trustee Investment (Scotland) Act 2005). Only organisations that meet this test can be registered on the Scottish Charity Register as charities under the law of Scotland.

The charity test will be met if:

- the organisation's purposes consist only of one or more of the charitable purposes listed in the 2005 Act; and
- the organisation provides public benefit in Scotland or elsewhere (or, for new applicants, intends to do so).

In determining whether an organisation seeking to be registered as a charity in Scotland meets the test, the Office of the Scottish Charity Regulator (OSCR) is required by the 2005 Act to 'have regard to' benefits to the organisation's members or others (in the capacity other than as a member of the public) and to any 'disbenefit' to the public.

The public benefit must outweigh any 'disbenefit' (the 2005 Act does not define this word).

There is no legal presumption of public benefit. The question of whether the legal criteria are met must be demonstrated on a case-by-case basis, in the context of the organisation's activities (or proposed activities, for a new organisation).

Scots law excludes an organisation from meeting this test if:

- its constitution allows its property to be applied for non-charitable purposes; or
- its constitution allows Scottish or UK Ministers to direct or otherwise control the organisation's activities; or
- the organisation has party political purposes.

In Northern Ireland, the Charities (Northern Ireland) Act 2008 provides that an organisation is a charity if:

- it is established for charitable purposes for the public benefit (the purposes must be within the list of purposes set out in the Act); and
- it is within the jurisdiction of the courts In Northern Ireland with regard to charities.

Charitable purposes: England and Wales (Charities Act 2011)

The Charities Act sets out descriptions of purposes *capable* of being charitable, in the right set of circumstances. Not every organisation with a relevant purpose will, in fact, be a charity. In addition, the lists are not definitive. The law is flexible, so that the legal meaning of 'charity' can develop as needs alter, society and social conditions change, and new means to provide charitable benefits evolve.

This list set out in the Act is as follows:

- The prevention or relief of poverty.
- The advancement of education.
- The advancement of religion. Religion can include:
  (i) a religion that involves belief in more than one god; and
  (ii) a religion that does not involve belief in a god.
- The advancement of health or the saving of lives. This includes the prevention or relief of sickness, disease or human suffering.
- The advancement of citizenship or community development. This can include rural or urban regeneration, and the promotion of civic responsibility, volunteering, the voluntary sector or the effectiveness or efficiency of charities.
- The advancement of the arts, culture, heritage or science.
- The advancement of amateur sport. This can include sport or games that promote health by involving physical or mental skill or exertion.
- The advancement of human rights, conflict resolution or reconciliation, or the promotion of religious or racial harmony, or equality and diversity.
- The advancement of environmental protection or improvement.
- The relief of those in need by reason of youth, age, ill-health, disability, financial hardship or other disadvantage. This can include relief given by the provision of accommodation or care to the relevant persons.
- The advancement of animal welfare.
- The promotion of the efficiency of the armed forces of the Crown, or of the efficiency of the police, fire and rescue services or ambulance services.
- Any other purposes that:
  (i) are not within 1–12 above but are recognised as charitable under section 5 of the 2011 Act (recreational and similar trusts) or under the old law (i.e. the law relating to charities in England and Wales in force immediately before 1 April 2008);
  (ii) are analogous to or within the spirit of 1–12 above;
  (iii) may reasonably be regarded as analogous to or within the spirit of any purposes which have been recognised, under the law relating to charities in England and Wales, as falling within (ii) above or this sub-paragraph (iii).

This 'sweeper' category is important in carrying forward all pre-existing charitable purposes not explicitly set out in the list. It also provides future flexibility so that the law can change and expand as society changes.

Recreational and similar trusts

Provision of facilities for recreation or leisure-time occupation, in the interests of social welfare, can be charitable, provided that these conditions are met:

(a) the facilities are provided with the object of improving the conditions of life for persons for whom the facilities are primarily intended;

(b) those persons have need of the facilities by reason of their youth, age, infirmity or disability, poverty or social and economic circumstances; or

(c) the facilities are to be available to the public at large or to male or female members of the public.

The Charities Act specifies that this applies in particular to village halls, community centres and women's institutes, as well as the provision and maintenance of grounds and buildings for recreation or leisure-time occupation, always subject to the requirement that the facilities are provided in the interests of social welfare.

The purposes of the specific organisation must be for the public benefit in order for it to qualify as a charity.

Community amateur sports clubs (registered sports clubs)

A 'registered sports club' is a club registered by Her Majesty's Revenue & Customs (HMRC) as an amateur sports club (known as a community amateur sports club or CASC). Such a club cannot be a charity.

Charitable purposes: Scotland

Charities and Trustee Investment (Scotland) Act 2005

The list of potentially charitable purposes for the charity test under the law of Scotland is as follows:

- The prevention or relief of poverty.
- The advancement of education.
- The advancement of religion.
- The advancement of health. This can include the prevention or relief of sickness, disease or human suffering.

- The saving of lives.
- The advancement of citizenship or community development. This can include rural or urban regeneration, and the promotion of civic responsibility, volunteering, the voluntary sector or the effectiveness or efficiency of charities.
- The advancement of the arts, heritage, culture or science.
- The advancement of public participation in sport (involving physical skill and exertion).
- The provision of recreational facilities, or organisation of recreational activities, with the object of improving the conditions of life for the persons for whom they are primarily intended. This applies only to recreational facilities or activities that are:
  - primarily intended for persons who have need of them because of their age, ill-health, disability, financial hardship or other disadvantage; or
  - available to members of the public at large or to male or female members of the public at large.
- The advancement of human rights, conflict resolution or reconciliation.
- The promotion of religious or racial harmony.
- The promotion of equality and diversity.
- The advancement of environmental protection or improvement.
- The relief of those in need by reason of age, ill-health, disability, financial hardship or other disadvantage. This can include relief given by the provision of accommodation or care.
- The advancement of animal welfare.
- Other purposes reasonably analogous to any of the purposes above. The advancement of any philosophical belief (whether or not involving belief in a god) can be analogous to the purpose set out at 3 above.

Charitable purposes: Northern Ireland

Charities (Northern Ireland) Act 2008

The list of potentially charitable purposes under the law of Northern Ireland is as follows:
- The prevention or relief of poverty.
- The advancement of education.

- The advancement of religion. 'Religion' includes:
  - a religion that involves belief in one god or more than one god; and
  - any analogous philosophical belief (whether or not involving belief in a god).
- The advancement of health or the saving of lives. The advancement of health includes the prevention or relief of sickness, disease or human suffering.
- The advancement of citizenship or community development. This includes rural or urban regeneration, and the promotion of civic responsibility, volunteering, the voluntary sector or the effectiveness or efficiency of charities.
- The advancement of the arts, culture, heritage or science.
- The advancement of amateur sport, i.e. sports or games that promote health by involving physical or mental skill or exertion.
- The advancement of human rights, conflict resolution or reconciliation, or the promotion of religious or racial harmony, or equality and diversity (this includes the advancement of peace and good community relations).
- The advancement of environmental protection or improvement.
- The relief of those in need by reason of youth, age, ill-health, disability, financial hardship or other disadvantage (this includes relief given by the provision of accommodation or care to the persons mentioned).
- The advancement of animal welfare.
- Any other existing purposes, and analogous purposes.

Charity essentials: charitable purposes, activities and outcomes for the public benefit

The individual charity's purposes are all-important. It is these purposes that the organisation must pursue for the public benefit and it may not lawfully go beyond its own purposes.

If a charity does go beyond its own purposes, this amounts to a breach of trust and can have serious legal consequences. These can include personal liability for the trustees, regardless of whether the charity has limited liability.

There is an important distinction between purposes and activities – advancing education is a purpose; running a school is an activity in pursuit of that educational purpose. The trustees have a prime responsibility to ensure the charity pursues appropriate activities in pursuit of its stated charitable purposes, in order to deliver relevant public benefit. Pursuing the specific charity's purposes for the public benefit is critical to retaining charitable status and is the very essence of what being a charity is all about.

Charities are therefore obliged to provide public benefit from their activities in pursuit of their charitable purposes and they must demonstrate how they do so.

Trustees and those involved in the governance and the legal administration of charities should be particularly careful to stay true to the charity's charitable purposes. It is important to guard against 'mission drift'.

Key consequences of charitable status

Having the legal status of being a charity has key consequences for the organisation, for its funds and assets and for the people involved in the organisation – any members (if it has a membership structure) and, particularly, its charity trustees. These key consequences include the following:

- The organisation is inherently outward focused.
- It must pursue its charitable purposes and provide charitable public benefit.
- Its funds and assets must be protected and used correctly, towards the charitable purposes and in accordance with charity law restrictions and requirements.
- No significant private or commercial benefits must arise from the organisation's activities.
- The organisation is regulated by charity law and overseen by the relevant charity regulator(s).
- It is publicly accountable and must provide detailed annual accounts and an annual trustees' report (unless it has specific exemptions from reporting obligations).
- The members have no commercial interests and they do not 'own' the charity, in the way that the members of a commercial company do.

- The trustees are stewards and custodians, with legal duties (in charitable incorporated organisations (CIOs) and Scottish charitable incorporated organisations (SCIOs) the members also have some legal duties).

Registration of charities

The obligation to register with the Charity Commission is a key legal consequence of being a charity under the law of England and Wales. The obligation applies unless the particular organisation is subject to an exception from the registration requirement, which many charities are (there are around 167,000 main registered charities on the register and the Charity Commission estimates that there are around 330,000 charities in total in England and Wales).

Failure to register when obliged to do so does not remove charitable status, but it is a breach of charity regulation.

The main reasons for formal legal exemption from charity registration are:

- the charity is beneath the registration income threshold (currently £5,000 annual income);
- the charity is legally 'excepted' from registration; or
- the charity is legally 'exempt' from registration.

Although charity law reforms were intended to remove 'excepted' and 'exempt' status from the vast majority of charities, this has only partially been achieved during a slow, and as yet incomplete, period of change.

Small charities

While there are arguably some benefits of being exempt from charity registration as a small charity (such as not having to file accounts and returns with the Charity Commission), there are very real practical disadvantages for these organisations, especially in relation to how they prove their charitable status. They are not listed on the register of charities and do not have a charity number. If a small charity has registered with HMRC for Gift Aid and other charity tax reliefs and exemptions, it will be given a charity tax reference number by HMRC. This may help it to demonstrate its charitable status to third parties.

Excepted charities

The main groups of 'excepted' charities are certain Christian religious charities (such as parochial church councils of financially smaller parish churches in the Church of England), scouts and guides and some armed forces charities. Historically, most of these were overseen by some other body (such as the national scouting and guiding bodies) although it is now recognised that this is not suitable for future regulatory oversight. This is one of the reasons for reforms proposing to remove almost all excepted status.

The largest formerly excepted organisations (annual income over £100,000) are now on the register of charities, but the rest await further registration phases, by income band. Theoretically the Charity Commission is the regulator of the unregistered remaining excepted charities and it can ask for information about their activities or investigate any that cause concern. It is hard to see how effective this oversight can be in practice, since an unregistered organisation is inevitably largely 'below the radar'.

Exempt charities

Exempt charities include many universities, various national museums and galleries, housing associations and charitable industrial and provident societies. As is the case for excepted charities, charity law reforms are bringing most of these on to the register and the largest are already registered (income over £100,000), with the rest awaiting further registration phases, by income band.

The exempt charities that are to retain exempt status are now overseen by a designated alternative principal regulator, not by the Charity Commission. Although such alternative principal regulators have a role of promoting compliance with charity law obligations, by the trustees of exempt charities, their prime focus is on the specific other areas of regulation for which they are responsible. In charity law matters, they do not have comparable powers to the Charity Commission.

Register of charities: England and Wales

The register of charities for England and Wales is kept by the Charity Commission.

Charity registration was first introduced by charity law reforms in the 1960s, although a comprehensive register of charities has still not been established, as many charities are not legally obliged to register. Voluntary registration is not an option in practice for these charities. Therefore, there are no details on the register of charities of 'excepted' charities, 'exempt' charities or small charities, beneath the income level for compulsory registration.

Only registrable charities governed by the law of England and Wales can be registered, so overseas organisations (including charities constituted under the law of Scotland) cannot register.

The information on the register of charities comes from the organisation's original charity registration application, its constitution and the annual reporting the charity must undertake to the Charity Commission.

The annual reporting documents are the main route by which changes come to the information on the register comes to the Commission's attention. By law, few changes have to be notified as they occur. However, the Commission encourages charities to notify key changes as they occur, especially changes among the trustees. It provides a simple online 'Update my charity' facility on its website for this purpose.

The entry for each charity is publicly accessible, via the Charity Commission's website, and provides details of:

- the name of the charity;
- the charity's contact details and the names of its trustees;
- the charitable purposes of the charity;
- a summary of its activities and where they are mainly carried out;
- the registered charity number;
- a summary of the charity's financial history and filing record;
- copies of annual accounts and trustees' reports (unless the charity is exempt from filing these because it is very small); and
- various other details, such as the constitutional form of the charity (i.e. its legal form).

Scottish Charity Register

The Scottish Charity Register is kept by the OSCR. It is a comprehensive register of every charity constituted under the law of Scotland or operating in Scotland (including charities constituted under some other legal system, including the law of England and Wales).

The entry for each charity is publicly accessible via the OSCR's website, and provides details of:

- the name of the charity;
- the charity's principal office address;
- the charitable purposes of the charity;
- a summary of its activities and where they are mainly carried out;
- the Scottish charity number; and
- various other details, such as the constitutional form of the charity (i.e. its legal form).

A link to the charity's latest accounts and trustees' report on the charity's website is also provided if the charity has provided it to OSCR.

Where it is necessary to protect an individual or the charity's premises, the address given may be the address of one of the trustees (this is rare).

The charity trustees are not listed on a charity's entry on the Scottish Charity Register. The OSCR is not obliged to keep a register of trustees and states that it does not have the resources to keep a list on a voluntary basis. Interested parties are advised by the OSCR to seek a copy of the annual accounts by contacting the charity directly, to ascertain who the trustees are.

The OSCR does not make full copies of the charity's constitution available on the register (this may change in the future).

The OSCR is obliged to ensure every organisation on the register meets the charity test. It must remove any organisation which does not do so and which fails to address the areas of concern, after having been given an opportunity to do so.

Other reasons for removal from the register include:

- voluntary removal at the request of the charity (steps would be required to protect any remaining charitable funds and assets before such a request could be granted);
- removal after amalgamation or winding-up (a formal legal process would be necessary to carry out either); or
- compulsory removal by the OSCR at the end of a statutory inquiry or because the organisation had failed to comply with the OSCR's monitoring requirements.

Register of charities: Northern Ireland

A comprehensive register of charities is being created and held by the Charity Commission for Northern Ireland, in accordance with the requirements of the Charities Act (Northern Ireland) 2008. The registration process is being managed in stages by the regulator, which is calling batches of charities forward for registration.

The register of charities in Northern Ireland can be accessed on the website of the Charity Commission for Northern Ireland.

Charity regulatory regime (England and Wales)

The general scheme of regulation for charities is public registration (unless one of the remaining exceptions or exemptions applies) regulatory oversight by the Charity Commission, and public accounting and reporting, on an annual basis.

The charity regulatory regime for England and Wales flows principally from the Charities Act 2011, supplemented by various regulations. The Act is a consolidating Act that did not make any substantial changes to the regulatory regime previously set out in the Charities Act 2006. However, there are some potentially confusing aspects to the regime and its legal underpinning by charity law as a whole, including the following:

- Some statutory provisions of charity law are still in older legislation (in particular the regulation of fundraising using professional fundraisers and the regulation of fundraising ventures with commercial organisations).
- There is no comprehensive charity registration regime for England and Wales, so the Charity Commission does not have complete jurisdiction over all charities.
- The Charities Act 2006 was subject to a statutory review requirement. This review was carried out after the 2011 Act had been placed on the statute book (in practice the review report does address charity law and the charity regulatory regime as now set out in the 2011 Act).
- The intended removal of most of the legal exceptions and exemptions from charity registration has made slow progress, with many of the charities affected still not able to become registered due to the

long drawn-out staged process of registration by income bands pursued by the Charity Commission.

Charity law itself is a mixture of common law, flowing from decisions of the courts, principal legislation (mainly the Charities Act 2011, with other important provisions flowing from the Charities (Protection and Social Investment) Act 2016) and secondary legislation (regulations set out in statutory instruments).

Role of the courts

All charities are subject to the ultimate supervision of the courts – the High Court in England and Wales, the Court of Session in Scotland and the High Court in Northern Ireland. The powers of the courts in relation to charities are aimed at protecting charitable assets and ensuring those assets are properly applied for the particular charitable purposes.

Day-to-day regulatory supervision of charities is undertaken by the three UK charity regulators: the Charity Commission, the Office of the Scottish Charity Regulator and the Charity Commission for Northern Ireland.

Role of the Upper Tribunal (England and Wales)

The Upper Tribunal (formerly called the 'Charity Tribunal') can:
- hear appeals against some decisions of the Charity Commission;
- hear applications for review of some decisions of the Charity Commission; and
- consider references from the Attorney General or the Charity Commission on points of law.

The Tribunal only has jurisdiction in respect of certain Charity Commission decisions made on or after 18 March 2008. These are specified in the Charities Act 2011.

An appeal can only be made to the Tribunal by a charity after that charity has used the Commission's own decision review process and a final decision has been issued on the matter in question by the Commission.

The Tribunal is independent of the Charity Commission and is part of HM Courts & Tribunals Service, an executive agency of the Ministry of Justice.

Details of the procedure for making an appeal are set out in regulations, and guidance is given on the Tribunal's website at www.charity.tribunals.gov.uk. The website also includes details of Tribunal decisions.

Role of the charity regulators

The prime role of the UK's three charity regulators is to ensure charitable funds and assets are protected and correctly applied, and that charities comply with their public accountability obligations, under the separate charity regulatory regimes applicable in England and Wales, Scotland and Northern Ireland. They do not police compliance with charity law and they cannot generally directly manage charities or intervene in the governance of charities by their trustee boards. Nor will they involve themselves in member disputes or issues of good governance (save where there is a particular need to intervene for the protection of charitable funds and assets considered to be at substantial risk).

Charity Commission: legal basis

The legal basis for the Charity Commission is set out in the Charities Act 2011. The Commission is a corporate body, with statutory objectives, functions and duties. It is independent of government and outside the direction or control of Ministers. It is accountable to Parliament through the Home Secretary and is ultimately answerable to the courts.

The Charity Commission's statutory objectives, functions and duties

The Charities Act 2011 gives the Charity Commission these objectives:
- To increase public trust and confidence in charities.
- To promote awareness and understanding of the public benefit requirement (i.e. the obligation for charities to provide public benefit).
- To promote compliance by charity trustees with their legal obligations in exercising control and management of the administration of their charities.
- To promote the effective use of charitable resources.
- To enhance the accountability of charities to donors, beneficiaries and the general public.

The Charity Commission's statutory functions are to:

- determine whether or not institutions are charities;
- encourage and facilitate the better administration of charities;
- identify and investigate the apparent misconduct or mismanagement in the administration of charities, and take remedial or protective action in connection with misconduct or mismanagement;
- determine whether public collection certificates should be issued and remain in force;
- obtain, evaluate and disseminate information in connection with the performance of the Commission's functions of the meeting of its objectives; and
- give information or advice, or make proposals, to Ministers, on matters relating to the Commission's functions or objectives.

It is because of item (a) that the Charity Commission is responsible for keeping the public Register of Charities in England and Wales. It also deals with new charity registrations. This is also the function under which the Charity Commission issues guidance on the public benefit test and monitors whether or not existing charities deliver suitable public benefit.

In addition, the Charity Commission has some general duties:

- To act in a way compatible with its objectives and most appropriate to meeting them.
- To act in a way compatible with the encouragement of charitable giving and voluntary participation in charity work.
- To have regard to the need to use its resources in the most efficient, effective and economic way.
- To have regard to the principles of best regulatory practice (including the principles under which regulatory activities should be proportionate, accountable, consistent, transparent and targeted only at cases in which action is needed).
- To have regard to the desirability of facilitating innovation by or on behalf of charities.
- To have regard to such generally accepted principles of good corporate governance as it is reasonable to regard as applicable to the Commission.

The Charity Commission has a range of specific statutory powers to protect charitable assets. However, it prefers to fulfil its protective role through encouraging charities to deal properly with their affairs in the first place, rather than having to use statutory intervention powers when serious problems have already occurred.

Inquiries

The Charity Commission can institute inquiries into charities (though it rarely does). An inquiry is a formal investigation and documents, information and written statements can be demanded from the charity or any individuals in relation to the inquiry. Information can also be obtained from other sources such as the police, local authorities and government departments. It is a criminal offence to give false or misleading information, and if necessary, statements on oath can be taken. Once an inquiry has been completed, the Charity Commission publishes its findings.

Intervention

The Commission has a range of powers of intervention. These divide into temporary protective powers and remedial powers:

- The temporary protective powers enable charity assets deemed to be at risk to be protected quickly. Charity trustees or employees can be suspended pending potential removal, additional trustees or a receiver and manager can be appointed, and transactions or property transfers can be made subject to Charity Commission prior approval.
- The remedial powers include removal of trustees or employees or the making of a scheme for the charity's administration. These may be used during an inquiry.

In both cases the Charity Commission can only act if it believes that there has been misconduct or mismanagement in the charity's administration and that the charity's property needs protection.

Discretionary power to disqualify trustees

The Charities (Protection and Social Investment) Act 2016 amended the Charities Act 2011 to introduce a discretionary power for the Charity Commission to disqualify trustees. This is in addition to the other disqualification provisions in charity law.

Before it can exercise this power, the regulator must be satisfied that three statutory criteria are met:

(a) at least one of the six conditions set out in the Charities Act has been met; and

(b) the individual is unfit to be a trustee; and

(c) a disqualification order is desirable in the public interest, in order to protect public trust and confidence in charities.

The six conditions (described as conditions A–F in the Charities Act) are:

(a) The person has been cautioned for an offence against a charity, or in the administration of a charity, that offence must be one for which a conviction would bring automatic disqualification.

(b) The person has been convicted of an offence in a country outside the UK that:
- is against a charity, or involves the administration of a charity; and
- if it had been committed in the UK, it would have been an offence which brought automatic disqualification from being a trustee.

(c) The person has been found by HMRC not to be a 'fit and proper person' to be a manager of a body or trust (under the relevant tax law provisions of the Finance Act 2010).

(d) The person was a trustee, officer, agent or employee of a charity and was responsible for, contributed to or facilitated misconduct or mismanagement in a charity, or the person knew of the misconduct or mismanagement and failed to take any reasonable step to oppose it.

(e) The person was an officer or employee of a corporate trustee who was responsible for, contributed to or facilitated misconduct or mismanagement in a charity, or the person knew of the misconduct or mismanagement and failed to take any reasonable step to oppose it.

(f) The person's past or continuing conduct, whether or not in relation to the charity, is, or is likely to, be damaging to public trust and confidence in a charity or charities.

With reference to condition A, cautions are formal warnings, given to a person who has admitted the relevant criminal offence before any prosecution occurs. Cautions issued before these statutory provisions came into force (i.e. before 1 October 2016) are within the scope of condition A.

With regard to condition F, the conduct does not have to be in the context of a charity. It might, for example, be in the person's professional or personal life.

The Commission's published explanatory statement on this discretionary disqualification power states that 'misconduct' includes any act (or failure to act) in the administration of a charity, where the person committing it knew (or ought to have known) that it was criminal, unlawful or improper.

With regard to 'mismanagement', the statement says that it includes any act (or failure to act) in the administration of a charity that may result in charitable resources being misused, or the beneficiaries of the charity being put at risk. The statement adds that 'a charity's reputation may be regarded as property of the charity'.

The exercise of this discretionary disqualification power is by order of the Charity Commission, a court hearing is not required. The period of disqualification is determined by the Commission (up to a maximum of 15 years).

Power to issue official warnings

Amendments introduced to the Charities Act 2011 by the Charities (Protection and Social Investment) Act 2016 provide a power for the Charity Commission to issue official warnings to charities or charity trustees. It can use this power if it considers there has been misconduct or mismanagement of the charity, or a breach of trust or breach of duty.

The Commission has issued guidance about its intended approach to use of this power. That guidance states that a period of prior notice of intention to issue a warning will be given, enabling the charity or trustee to respond. The guidance also states that when the Commission issues an official warning it will decide, on a case-by-case basis, whether to publish that warning.

There is no right of appeal to the Charity Tribunal against an official warning issued by the Charity Commission.

Additional Charity Commission powers

The Charity Commission has a number of additional powers, including the following:

- Subject to certain conditions being met, it can grant relief from liability for breach of trust or breach of duties to trustees, by an order. The power (which will only rarely be exercised) is available if the Commission considers the trustees acted honestly and reasonably and ought fairly to be excused from the breach.
- The Commission has power to waive the disqualification of any former trustee after a five-year period.
- The Commission has power to give formal advice to charities (but it rarely does so).
- The Commission has power to determine the membership of a membership charity, in cases of doubt. This can be done when a formal inquiry has been opened or at the request of the charity itself.
- The Commission has power to direct the transfer of funds in a charity bank account that has been dormant for five or more years to another suitable charity.
- The Commission can enter premises and seize documents or information, under the authority of a warrant. This can be used when a formal inquiry has been opened.

Regulatory monitoring of charities

The charity regulators use the documents that charities must file every year as a key tool in monitoring charities (i.e. charity annual returns and annual accounts and trustees' reports). This monitoring is designed to ensure charities are complying with regulatory requirements, especially those relating to annual filing of documents on to the public record held by the relevant regulator(s) for each charity, and to ensure charities are reporting within the statutory time limits.

The monitoring is also intended to detect areas of potential concern. For this purpose, the Charity Commission's staff use certain 'triggers' – particular matters that may give rise to concerns and lead to further scrutiny or correspondence and discussions with the particular charity. Triggers include:

- improper and unauthorised payments to or other benefits for trustees;
- unauthorised and improper dealings between the charity and trustees or individuals/organisations 'connected' with trustees; and

- unsecured loans to trading subsidiaries or other apparently improper trading activities.

More detailed scrutiny is given to the documents filed by larger charities.

Monitoring: charity annual returns, annual accounts and reports

The contents of charity annual returns and the annual accounts and trustees' reports filed by charities are particularly important in the monitoring regimes operated by the charity regulators in England and Wales and Scotland. Both regulators concentrate on certain matters, such as the correct application of funds and assets, unauthorised benefits for trustees and persons connected with them, or improper trading activities.

Both regulators place particular emphasis on timely filing of these items, and correct contents (in accordance with the legal reporting obligations applicable to the charity in question). They encourage charities to comply with their obligations and offer useful guidance notes and other general advice to assist (available on the regulators' websites).

Monitoring: public benefit and charitable assets

The Charity Commission is obliged to review the register of charities, to ensure organisations on that register remain charitable in law, and to monitor the public benefit charities provide. Most of the Commission's work in these areas is done through monitoring and careful analysis of all documents and returns filed by a charity to meet its legal reporting and accounting obligations.

Well-organised and well-governed charities, with adequate records and good practices, should have nothing to fear from these monitoring processes – the Commission will simply see the good that is already there.

Charity regulatory regime (Scotland)

The general scheme of regulation for charities in Scotland is comprehensive public registration on the Scottish Charity Register (there are no exemptions from registration), regulatory oversight by the OSCR, and public accounting and reporting, on an annual basis.

The charity regulatory regime for Scotland flows principally from the Charities and Trustee Investment (Scotland) Act 2005, supplemented by various regulations.

The OSCR has broadly similar functions and powers to those of the Charity Commission, including intervention and investigation powers intended to safeguard charitable funds and assets.

As well as organisations constituted under the law of Scotland, any charitable organisation constituted under the law of another legal system (including the law of England and Wales) must register if the organisation:

- is managed or controlled wholly or mainly in Scotland; or
- occupies land or premises in Scotland; or
- carries out activities in any office, shop or similar premises in Scotland.

The OSCR has issued guidance on its website (www.oscr.org.uk) explaining how it interprets these conditions and indicating the circumstances in which a relevant organisation should apply for registration.

Regulatory consents: Scotland

A charity on the Scottish Charity Register must obtain the OSCR's prior consent for:

- amending the charitable purposes in its constitution;
- amalgamating with another body;
- winding-up or dissolving; or
- making a court application in relation to any of the above.

The charity must give the OSCR at least 42 days' notice of the proposed action. An amendment to the charitable purposes in the constitution must not be dealt with until the required consent has been formally given.

For other matters, unless within 28 days of the notification to the OSCR by the charity, the OSCR has refused consent or has directed the charity not to take the requested action for six months, the charity can assume the OSCR consents and proceed.

Notification of changes to the OSCR: Scotland

A charity on the Scottish Charity Register must notify the OSCR of the following changes:

- a change to its principal office;
- a change to any of the charity's other registered details;
- a change to the constitution (which also requires the OSCR's prior consent);

- any action in relation to an amalgamation, winding-up, dissolution or application to the court with regard to any of those matters (these also require the OSCR's prior consent);
- the making of a court order for the administration or winding-up of the charity; or
- the appointment of a receiver in respect of any of the charity's property.

This must be done within three months of the date of the change or in relation to the making of a court order for administration or winding-up or the appointment of a receiver, within one month of that event.

Charity regulatory regime (Northern Ireland)

The general scheme of regulation for charities in Northern Ireland is based on public registration on the Northern Ireland Charity Register, regulatory oversight by the Charity Commission for Northern Ireland, and public accounting and reporting, on an annual basis.

The charity regulatory regime for Northern Ireland flows principally from the Charities Act (Northern Ireland) 2008 and supplementary regulations.

The Charity Commission for Northern Ireland has broadly similar functions and powers to those of the Charity Commission in England and Wales, including intervention and investigation powers intended to safeguard charitable funds and assets.

Main legal forms used by charities

Charities may take a wide variety of legal forms. Some forms are specific to charitable status and cannot be used by non-charities – for example, the charitable incorporated organisation (CIO) and its Scottish equivalent (Scottish charitable incorporated organisation, SCIO) and the Northern Ireland equivalent (also called the charitable incorporated organisation). Other legal forms, such as unincorporated members' organisations or companies, are available to and used by non-charities as well as charities. The three most common legal forms used by charities (prior to the introduction of the CIO/SCIO) were:

- unincorporated charitable trust;
- unincorporated members' association; and
- company limited by guarantee.

Key features of the most common legal forms

The key features of the most common legal forms used by charities are described below.

Trust

Under the law of England and Wales, a trust has no independent legal identity. It therefore does not exist as a separate entity in its own right and so does not have its own legal capacity (e.g. to enter into contracts or hold property directly).

A trust has no formal legal membership; there are simply trustees. Those trustees do not have limited liability protection.

A charitable trust is subject to the general principles of trust law, but above all it is subject to charity law.

A trust is typically the legal form taken by a long-established historic grant-making charity that has no direct other activities of its own and is a relatively low-risk operation. However, given rising anxiety about the potential liabilities of charity trustees, as well as the difficulties of holding assets via nominees, new grant-making charities often choose an incorporated legal form instead.

Unincorporated members' association

An unincorporated members' association is a group of individuals associating together for a common purpose; in the case of a charity that will be the charitable purpose set out in the constitution. It has no independent legal identity. It therefore does not exist as a separate entity in its own right and so does not have its own legal capacity (e.g. to enter into contracts or hold property directly).

As is the case with a trust, this gives rise to legal and practical difficulties in holding and dealing with assets, and entering into contracts and other legal arrangements.

The association has a formal membership and also a group of trustees (usually, but not necessarily, the trustees are drawn from among a wider membership).

Neither the trustees nor the members are protected by limited liability.

An unincorporated members' association is heavily dependent on its own constitution. The law regulating such associations is largely common law and has been little developed by statute.

As such organisations do not have their own distinct legal identity and do not provide limited liability protection, a number of difficulties are inherent. These include the following:

- The association cannot enter into contracts or other legal agreements in its own capacity – the officers must do so in their personal capacities (with attendant personal liabilities).

- The association cannot be held liable for wrongful acts committed by its representatives while acting on its behalf. This gives rise to personal liability risks for the individuals in question. Worse, it remains unclear in law how far liability can extend to all the officers or even the general membership of the association – especially if the association's assets are insufficient to meet relevant liabilities to a third party.

- A member cannot sue for damages for injury sustained as a consequence of the wrongful act of an officer or fellow member acting on the association's behalf.

- The association cannot own property, so individual members or officers have to hold the title in a trustee capacity. Title transfers are therefore necessary when personnel change.

Charitable company

A charitable company does have its own independent legal identity. So it can have and enforce legal rights and is responsible for its own legal commitments, as well as its own debts and liabilities.

It has trustees (who are also directors for company law purposes) and it must also have some formal members. There can be complete or partial commonality between the board and the membership or no overlap (subject to the terms of the charity's articles).

Members and trustees are protected by limited liability under normal circumstances.

A charitable company has statutory power (flowing from the Companies Act 2006) to do anything lawful in pursuit of its charitable purposes. Those purposes will be set out in its articles (which are its constitution).

Company law provides a clear legal framework for a charitable company (Companies Act 2006 and association regulations) alongside charity law.

A charitable company is subject to the company regulatory regime, which is modified for charitable companies because of their charitable status and the requirements of charity regulations. This does not impose significant additional burdens, as the annual accounts and trustees' report prepared for submission to the Charity Commission can also be filed with Companies House. The only additional item required is a company annual return form, which is a simple document and can be filed quickly and easily online via Companies House website (using the WebFiling facility).

New legal forms available to charities

The new legal forms introduced for charities recently are the charitable incorporated organisation (CIO) and the Scottish equivalent (Scottish charitable incorporated organisation, SCIO). In due course the new Northern Ireland equivalent will also be introduced (also called the charitable incorporated organisation).

These are optional legal forms, introducing further choice to the range of legal forms already available. They may be suitable for some circumstances but will not be the appropriate choice for all charities.

No pre-existing charity has any obligation to convert to a CIO or SCIO.

CIO

The main legal features of a CIO are as follows:

- It is a corporate body (so it has independent legal identity and its own legal capacity).
- It is a membership organisation, so there must be at least one formal member, as well as trustees.
- It provides limited liability protection to its members and trustees (under normal circumstances, this can be removed – for example, if there is a breach of trust by the trustees).
- It is only available to charities (it cannot be used by non-charities).
- It is established by registration with the Charity Commission (not Companies House).

A CIO's assets are subject to a trust, for use in furtherance of its charitable purposes and in accordance with its constitution. This adds a certain degree of legal complexity to the arrangements a CIO can make regarding its property and how it may deal with that property.

A CIO has statutory power to do anything that is calculated to further its charitable purposes. Those purposes will be set out in its constitution.

A CIO cannot register charges it creates on the register of charities, unlike a charitable company that can (and indeed must) register charges it creates on the register of companies held by Companies House. This may cause some practical difficulties for a CIO that needs to create security (e.g. to acquire a property or secure borrowings).

A CIO's members are subject to a statutory duty to further the CIO's purposes. There is no comparable duty for the members of other legal forms of charity (except a SCIO).

Certain decisions must be taken by resolution of the members.

A CIO that uses the Charity Commission 'association' model constitution must hold an annual general meeting (AGM) of its members at least once in every 15 months (the first AGM must be held within 18 months of the registration of the CIO). Note that this is not a statutory obligation; it only arises if the particular CIO's constitution requires an AGM to be held.

There are detailed rules about the contents of CIO constitutions.

CIOs are subject to CIO-specific provisions in the Charities Act, to general charity law and to supplementary CIO-specific regulations. The regulations impose a range of requirements regarding names, disclosure of their charitable and CIO status, legal administration, statutory registers, record-keeping and public accountability.

CIOs are obliged to file annual accounts and reports with the Charity Commission (regardless of income level).

A CIO must have a principal office in England and Wales. This is its official address and fulfils a function comparable to the registered office of a company.

CIOs may amalgamate with *other CIOs*. CIOs may transfer their undertakings to *other CIOs*.

However, CIOs cannot specifically convert into alternative legal forms (more complex restructuring might be possible, depending on the particular circumstances), so care should be taken in deciding if the CIO legal form is right for the individual charity before applying to register a CIO.

SCIO

The main legal features of SCIOs are broadly similar to those of CIOs.

SCIOs are established by applying to the OSCR for registration on the Scottish Charity Register (not to Companies House).

A SCIO must meet the charity test at its registration and must continue to do so throughout its existence. Continued registration, and thus continued existence and charitable status, is dependent on this.

There are a number of SCIO-specific requirements and restrictions, in a number of areas, including:

- names;
- duties of the SCIO's members;
- required disclosures and references to charitable status (in documents and communications etc, including e-mails and websites);
- keeping registers and making certain information from them available on request;
- holding regular meetings of the members;
- amalgamation with other bodies;
- transfer of undertaking to another organisation; and
- dissolution and winding up.

A SCIO must have a principal office in Scotland. This is its official address and fulfils a function comparable to the registered office of a company.

Certain decisions must be taken by resolution of the members.

A SCIO must hold a meeting of its members at least once every 15 months. Note there is no opt-out available (unlike charitable companies, which are only obliged to hold AGMs if their own articles require them to do so). This will be an irritating administrative burden for those SCIOs that have a commonality of members and trustees.

There are particular requirements for the contents of SCIO constitutions.

The usual governance, transparency and accountability standards for charities apply to SCIOs. They are subject to annual accounting and reporting obligations; members of the public may ask to see a copy of their annual accounts and trustees' report.

Note that the SCIO legislation does not specifically address conflicts of interest (unlike company law). Instead, the relevant SCIO regulations require a SCIO's own constitution to include appropriate clauses.

Statutory registers must be kept by a SCIO and must be up to date. These include a register of members and a register of trustees.

A SCIO can only amalgamate with another new SCIO (not with an existing SCIO and not with any other type of charity).

If two SCIOs wish to combine, that has to be done as a winding-up of one and the transfer of its assets to the other. (This is because the SCIO amalgamation rules only permit amalgamation to be done by two or more existing SCIOs ceasing to exist and a new SCIO coming into being.)

The OSCR's consent is needed in advance before a SCIO can do certain things and make certain changes.

2 Constitution: the governing document

Constitution: general

A charity's constitution is its governing document, sometimes called the governing instrument. It specifies the charitable purposes and sets the framework for the governance of the organisation. The constitution will also contain at least some provisions concerning the internal administration of the charity.

Form and contents of the constitution

The form and contents of a charity's constitution depend on:
- the legal form of the charity (trust, members' association, charitable company, CIO, etc);
- core charity law principles (for example, relating to charitable purposes and charitable funds and assets);
- any specific legal or regulatory rules applicable because of the nature of the purposes and activities of the specific organisation; and
- the choices made by the members when adopting the constitution (in a membership charity) or the original founders or current trustees (in a trust).

Name of the constitution

The name of the constitution varies depending on the legal form of the particular charity.

Table 1: The name of the constitution according to the type of charity

Type of charity	Name of constitution
Trust	Trust deed, declaration of trust or trust document
Charitable company	Articles of association
Members' association	Constitution or rules
CIO or SCIO	Constitution
Industrial and provident society	Rules

Notes

1 A charitable trust may have been created under the terms of a will.
2 Companies incorporated prior to 1 October 2009 had a two-part constitution (memorandum and articles of association). The Companies Act 2006 provides that the memorandum of an old company is now to be treated as part of its articles. An old company may have modernised its constitution to incorporate both parts into one single new set of articles to supersede its previous memorandum and articles (all the provisions of the former memorandum that remain effective will have been moved into the new articles). There is no obligation to alter the memorandum and articles in this way, although it is a helpful way to modernise old companies' articles.
3 Articles of association are often simply described as articles.

Constitution: trustees' duties

The trustees must ensure the charity operates within its constitution and does not go beyond its charitable purposes or any limits on its powers set out in the constitution. Failure to do so could lead to potential liabilities for breach of duties or even for a breach of trust.

When using any charity's constitutional powers or the board's powers that flow from the charity's constitution, the trustees must satisfy themselves that the proposed course of action is in the charity's best interests.

For the trustees of a charitable company, there is a specific statutory duty for its directors to:

(a) act in accordance with the company's constitution; and
(b) only exercise their powers for the purposes for which those powers are conferred (i.e. the powers given to the trustees by, or available to the trustees from, the constitution).

(See section 171 of the Companies Act 2006.)

In carrying out or authorising an action by the company, the trustees must be satisfied that:

- the company has the capacity to do what is proposed and is not restricted by its constitution in relation to the action;
- the trustees themselves have authority to exercise the power; and
- they are exercising it for the purpose for which it was conferred by the constitution.

The trustees of other legal forms of charities should exercise similar caution when proposing to use the charity's constitutional powers. They should also be mindful as to whether the charity itself has powers, which they are exercising on its behalf, or whether they are acting in a personal capacity because the charity does not have its own legal capacity (e.g. a charitable trust or an unincorporated members' association).

Impact and importance of the constitution

A charity must be governed and operated in accordance with its constitution, at all times. The constitution is of fundamental importance and the trustees must ensure they are familiar with it and that senior staff, officers and key volunteers understand the key aspects of the constitution.

Constitution is king in most matters – for example, if the constitution demands the appointment of an auditor and audit of the annual accounts or, in a charitable company, if its articles require the holding of an annual general meeting, that requirement must be observed (if they are silent, the AGM is optional). However, there are areas in which the law overrides the constitution. Some examples include:

- statutory accounting and reporting obligations;
- deadlines for submission of annual accounts and reports, charity annual returns and, for charitable companies, company annual returns to relevant regulators;
- statutory obligations to obtain regulatory consents (for example, to a proposed alteration to the charitable purposes); and

- fundamental rights of company members in charitable companies (such as the right to receive copies of the annual accounts and reports or the right to appoint proxies to attend and vote at general meetings).

Effectiveness of the constitution

The original constitution of a new organisation takes effect as that organisation comes into being. Subsequent alterations may take effect immediately or they may require registration before they take legal effect. Certain alterations will have no legal effect unless required prior consent to those changes has been obtained from the relevant charity regulator(s) (see further comments on alterations later in this chapter).

The constitution generally remains effective unless and until it is altered or the charity changes into an alternative legal form, in which case the new constitution of the successor charity must be observed in relation to that new charity (the constitution of the predecessor charity does not apply to the new organisation).

Reviewing the constitution

It is advisable to review the charity's constitution periodically (every three to five years as a rule of thumb) because law and practice change, governance standards develop and the charity's situation (as well as the wider social context in which it operates) will change over time. Particular triggers for review and change, in between regular reviews, may include:

- restructuring of the charity;
- significant legal changes, especially in charity law;
- significant growth of the charity or major expansion of its operations;
- proposals to remove or reduce unnecessarily restrictive limits on the charity's powers;
- difficulties in pursuing the charitable purposes, which may be too narrow or no longer easily addressed due to social change, economic factors or other external issues; and
- proposals to change the way in which the charity operates, so it can be more effective in pursuing its purposes for the public benefit (its current constitution may restrict or prevent the intended new activities).

Alterations to the constitution

Most aspects of a charity's constitution can be altered, although the prior consent of the relevant charity regulator(s) will be needed for some alterations, especially alterations to the charitable purposes or to the dissolution provisions.

The legal and administrative steps involved in making an alteration will vary depending on the charity's legal form.

In membership charities, a formal decision of the members will be required to alter the constitution; the trustees will not have power to make changes to the constitution by their own decision. Where the trustees are the only members of the charity, it is important to ensure they are aware of this and act in the correct capacity with regard to changes to the charity's constitution.

Most alterations take immediate effect, when the members pass the necessary resolution; however:

- changes that require prior consent from one or more charity regulators will not normally be effective unless that consent has been obtained;
- changes to CIO constitutions do not take effect until the Charity Commission registers them on the register of charities (this applies to all changes); and
- changes to a charitable company's charitable purposes do not take effect until the Registrar of Companies adds them to the particular company's entry on the register of companies (other changes do take immediate effect, subject to any required prior regulatory consent).

It is important to retain up-to-date copies of the constitution at the charity's office for reference, including all amendments currently in force. The charity should also ensure up-to-date copies are provided to professional advisers, the charity's auditor or independent examiner and any other relevant third parties (such as the charity's bank and its major funders).

When changes are made to a charity's constitution, a copy of that altered constitution should be provided to the Charity Commission together with a copy of the relevant resolution that effected the changes (these items must be sent to the Commission if the charity is a CIO). A charity on the Scottish Charity Register must notify the OSCR of all changes and provide copies of the altered constitution within three months of the date of the changes.

Further details about the legal process for altering the constitutions of particular types of charity are set out later in this chapter.

Trusts

Charitable trusts can be established by will, in which case the terms of the trust take effect on the death of the testator and the relevant provisions of the will act as the initial constitution. Alternatively, they may be established during the founder's lifetime, by a declaration or deed of trust. That document is the initial constitution of the trust.

Some older charitable trusts were established by trust provisions in another legal document, for example, a conveyance of land on trust for charitable purposes.

Trust law provides some of the governance framework for trusts and certain statutory powers for the trustees, but much of their governance and many of the trustees' powers are derived from their individual trust documents.

The charitable purposes will be set out in the trust document. This will usually also provide for:

- minimum and any maximum number of trustees (the Charity Commission regards a minimum of three as good practice);
- appointment of trustees (including any eligibility criteria), terms of office and cessation of office;
- trustees' powers;
- procedures for meetings of the trustees;
- various administrative powers for the management of the trust and its property;
- alteration of the trust document (subject to limitations and required regulatory consents – for instance, consent from the relevant charity regulator(s) to alteration of the charitable purposes); and
- dissolution of the trust and transfer of its assets to similar charitable purposes.

Alteration of a trust document

Generally the trust document includes a power of amendment. This will provide power for the trustees to make at least some changes by decision of the board (other formalities may be required such as the signature of a deed of alteration). Certain alterations, such as changes to the charitable trusts themselves, will require prior consent from the relevant charity regulator(s).

If the document does not provide a suitable power of amendment (changes may be limited to merely administrative matters, rather than substantive alterations), the statutory powers provided by the Charities Act may be available (see further comments later in this chapter).

Unincorporated members' associations

Unincorporated members' associations are heavily dependent on the terms of their individual constitutions. While there are certain legal principles, flowing from common law, that impact on the constitutions of such associations, there are no specific statutory provisions about the content of their constitutions.

The charitable purposes will be set out in the constitution. This will usually also provide for:

- minimum and any maximum number of trustees (the Charity Commission regards a minimum of three as good practice);
- appointment of trustees (including any eligibility criteria), terms of office and cessation of office;
- trustees' powers;
- admission to and cessation of membership;
- members' rights and obligations;
- procedures for meetings of the trustees and of the members;
- various administrative powers for the management of the association;
- provisions for the holding and management of assets for the association's charitable purposes;
- alteration of the constitution (subject to limitations and required regulatory consents – for instance, consent from the relevant charity regulator(s) to alteration of the charitable purposes); and
- dissolution of the organisation and transfer of its assets to similar charitable purposes.

Alteration of the constitution

Generally the constitution of an unincorporated members' association includes a power of amendment. This will usually provide for changes to be made by resolution of the members, passed at a members' meeting called on a particular period of notice. There will be a specified majority vote required for that resolution to be passed (typically two-thirds of the total membership voting in favour or two-thirds of the votes actually cast at the meeting).

As with other legal forms of charity, certain alterations, such as changes to the charitable purposes, will require prior consent from the relevant charity regulator(s).

If the document does not provide any power of amendment, the statutory powers provided by the Charities Act may be available (see further comments later in this chapter).

Charitable companies

Charitable companies must include certain provisions in their articles, in particular:

- the charitable purposes; and
- the name of the company.

A statement of limited liability and details of the members' guarantee are no longer required in the articles of new companies (incorporated under the Companies Act 2006) but are sometimes included for information. Other matters to address include:

- membership eligibility and provisions for the admission of members and cessation of membership (the statutory minimum number of members is one, but the articles can, and often do, set this at a higher level – typically three);
- provisions for the appointment (including any eligibility criteria), terms of office and cessation of office of the trustees;
- the minimum number of trustees (the Charity Commission regards three as good practice) and any maximum number (if applicable);
- powers of the trustees (this may be a general statement that the trustees can manage the charity and exercise all its powers);
- procedural rules including rules for meetings (of members and of trustees);

- empowering provisions, enabling the company to make the fullest use of electronic communications with its members permitted by the Companies Act 2006 (at the option of the company and, where necessary, subject to the members' actual or deemed consent);
- provisions for use of a seal, if the company may opt to have a seal (it does not have to have a seal and it does not have to use the seal even where it has adopted one, as alternative methods of executing specific documents may be used); and
- winding-up provisions, including directions about the application of the company's property for similar charitable purposes.

Alteration of the articles

A charitable company can alter its articles by special resolution of its members, passed either at a general meeting or by written resolution (using the statutory written resolution procedure set out in the Companies Act 2006 – see sections 288–300). If it is to be considered at a meeting, the resolution can be considered at the annual general meeting or at a general meeting convened specifically to deal with the proposed alteration of the articles.

A charitable company must obtain the Charity Commission's prior consent to a regulated alteration (section 198(2) of the Charities Act 2011). The change is ineffective if this consent is not obtained.

Regulated alterations are:

- changes to the charitable purposes;
- alteration to provide benefits for trustees or connected persons; and
- alterations to any provisions that direct how the company's property is to be applied on its dissolution.

For charitable companies registered on the Scottish Charity Register, consent of the OSCR must be obtained for a change to the charitable purposes or to the dissolution provisions.

A certified copy of the special resolution, with a copy of the altered articles, must be filed at Companies House (and a form CC04: Change of Objects if the charitable purposes are being altered).

An alteration to the charitable purposes of a charitable company does not take effect until the Registrar of Companies has registered the relevant documents on the register of companies (see section 31(2)(c) of the Companies Act 2006). Other changes take effect on the passing of the resolution (subject to any required prior regulatory consents having been obtained from relevant charity regulators).

Charities Act power to alter constitutions (unincorporated charities)

Where the constitution of an unincorporated charity does not provide a specific power of amendment, it may be possible for the trustees to use one of the statutory powers of amendment provided by the Charities Act 2011 (sections 275 and 280). These are not available if the charity holds land given for its charitable purposes (or part of those purposes).

The trustees of a small charity (with an annual income under £10,000) may alter the charitable purposes of the charity provided the trustees are satisfied that:

- it is expedient in the interests of the charity for its current purposes to be replaced; and
- so far as reasonably practicable, the proposed new purposes are similar to those they will replace.

For a membership charity, the trustees would need to satisfy themselves on these points and then obtain approval of the changes by the members (a two-thirds majority in favour of the proposal is required).

Copies of the relevant resolutions and a statement from the trustees, providing their reasons for making the changes, must be provided to the Charity Commission. The Commission can require the proposed changes to be advertised or, if it does not think the changes are appropriate, it can prevent them from becoming effective. Otherwise, the changes will take effect 60 days after the documents are provided to the Commission.

The trustees of an unincorporated charity may alter the constitution in relation to their administrative powers and procedures (no income threshold applies). The trustees must satisfy themselves on the two points listed above before exercising this power. The change takes immediate effect, as the resolution is passed; however, it must be notified to the Charity Commission. This power is useful for making practical administrative alterations, such as changes to the quorum required for trustees' meetings.

Orders and schemes

It is now rare to have to seek a Charity Commission order or revisions to a scheme to make changes to the constitution of an unincorporated charity, as the alternative powers in the Charities Act (described above) are usually available to deal with most relatively minor changes. However, if the charity has land subject to trusts or there are other forms of legal restrictions applicable to the charity's assets (endowment provisions or other special trusts) the Charities Act powers will not be sufficient and the process of change will be more legally complex. It may then be necessary to seek a formal order or scheme, agreed with the Charity Commission. In such situations, legal advice should be taken.

Charitable incorporated organisations (CIOs)

The Charity Commission is empowered to make regulations for CIO constitutions and has done so (see the Charities Act 2011 (Charitable Incorporated Organisations) (Constitutions) Regulations 2012).

A CIO's constitution must either be in a form specified by the Charity Commission (i.e. one of the Commission's model CIO constitutions, as set out in the regulations) or 'as near to that form as the circumstances allow'. In practice, the wording is not prescribed, so a CIO can have a custom drafted constitution, provided the document contains all the features specifically required by the Charities Act and the CIO regulations.

These matters must be included in a CIO's constitution:
- the name of the CIO;
- its charitable purposes;
- whether its principal office is in England or Wales (it is not necessary to set out the full address);
- whether or not its members are liable to contribute to its assets if it is wound up and, if they are, up to what amount;
- membership eligibility and provisions for the admission of members and cessation of membership (the statutory minimum number of members is one, but the constitution could set this at a higher level);
- provisions for the appointment and cessation of office of the trustees (and any eligibility criteria for appointment);

- if the minimum number of trustees is more than one (as is both likely and advisable, the Charity Commission regards three as good practice), the minimum number must be stated;
- if the trustees are to have power to take decisions by resolutions in writing, or by electronic means outside board meetings, relevant provisions must be included for that;
- for a new CIO, the constitution must list the names of the first trustees;
- procedural rules including rules for meetings (of members and of trustees);
- proxy rights for members, if they are to have such rights (the rights are not automatic as they would be in a charitable company);
- postal voting rights for members, if they are to have such rights;
- provisions for automatic use of electronic communications or a website to communicate formally with its members, if it intends to do that;
- provisions for use of the seal, if the CIO is to have one (the CIO may but does not have to have a seal); and
- directions about the application of the CIO's property on its dissolution for similar charitable purposes.

Although it is not a requirement to make provisions about the appointment of officers in the CIO's constitution, it is clearly wise to do so. At the very least, a CIO will need to appoint a chairman of its board of trustees. It may also wish to appoint a treasurer and/or secretary, and possibly other officers, such as a vice-chairman.

As with charities in other legal forms, it is good governance practice (but not a legal requirement) for the constitution of a CIO to provide that trustees serve specified limited terms of office.

A CIO's constitution must be in English if its principal office is in England. If the principal office is in Wales, the constitution may be in either English or Welsh.

The Charity Commission has produced two model CIO constitutions: the 'foundation' model for CIOs, in which members and trustees are the same people, and the 'association' model for CIOs that have a membership wider than the trustee board. Use of these models is optional.

Alteration of a CIO's constitution

An alteration to a CIO's constitution may only be made by decision of its members. A 75% majority of the votes cast is required if the relevant resolution is proposed at a general meeting; unanimity is required if the decision is taken in writing.

If the proposed alteration is a change to the charitable purposes or would authorise benefits to trustees or connected persons, or alters the dissolution provisions, the prior consent of the Charity Commission is required.

A copy of the resolution approving the changes and a copy of the amended constitution must be sent to the Charity Commission within 15 working days from the date of the resolution.

Regardless of the nature of the alteration, it does not take effect until the Charity Commission has recorded it in the register of charities. This is an important difference from the position for other legal forms of charities, where alterations normally take immediate effect (except for alteration of the charitable purposes of a charitable company which take effect when the Registrar of Companies registers the required documents on the register of companies).

Conversion to a CIO

Existing charities may convert to the CIO legal form, usually by setting up a new CIO as successor to the present charity and transferring the original charity's assets to that new CIO.

Additional regulations to address conversion of charitable companies to CIOs have not yet been made.

Once an organisation has become a CIO, it cannot usually convert itself into an alternative legal form later. It could in the future transfer its undertaking to another CIO or amalgamate with another CIO, subject to consent from the Charity Commission (but not amalgamate with any other type of charity).

The legal, administrative and practical issues involved in a conversion will vary according to the circumstances and the current legal form of the converting charity. Professional advice should be taken.

Scottish charitable incorporated organisations (SCIOs)

A SCIO's governing document is its constitution. The constitution can be created specifically to suit the individual SCIO's circumstances, provided it includes rules on certain areas, including:

- the name of the SCIO;
- its charitable purposes;
- any optional additional restrictions on the SCIO's powers (beyond those that are mandatory by law);
- organisational structure;
- board composition;
- office bearers (i.e. what office bearers the SCIO has and how they are appointed);
- procedural rules including rules for meetings (of members and of trustees);
- membership eligibility and provisions for the admission, withdrawal and removal of members;
- eligibility for trusteeship and provisions for the appointment and cessation of office of the charity trustees;
- any optional additional restrictions on the remuneration of trustees (beyond those in the Charities and Trustee Investment (Scotland) Act);
- procedures for dealing with conflicts of interest; and
- a requirement for surplus funds on winding-up to be transferred to similar charitable purposes.

Note there are no prescribed statutory model constitutions for SCIOs and the OSCR has not issued any models.

Alteration of a SCIO's constitution

An alteration to a SCIO's constitution may only be made by decision of its members. A two-thirds majority vote is required if the relevant resolution is proposed at a general meeting; unanimity is required if the decision is taken by some other means such as a written decision.

If the proposed alteration is a change to the charitable purposes or to the dissolution provisions, the prior consent of the OSCR is required.

The OSCR must be notified of all changes to a SCIO's constitution within three months of the date on which these were made, whether or not those changes required its prior consent.

Alterations to SCIO constitutions take immediate effect (in the case of an alteration to the charitable purposes, this is provided that the OSCR's prior consent was obtained). This is different to the position for CIOs in England and Wales, where alterations are not effective until the Charity Commission registers the changes.

Conversion to a SCIO

Existing charities may convert to the SCIO legal form, including unincorporated trusts and members' associations, charitable companies and charitable industrial and provident societies. The OSCR's prior consent is needed.

Once the organisation has become a SCIO by conversion, it cannot usually convert itself into an alternative legal form later. It could in the future transfer its undertaking to another SCIO or amalgamate with another SCIO, subject to consent from the OSCR (but not amalgamate with any other type of charity).

The legal, administrative and practical issues involved in a conversion will vary according to the circumstances and the current legal form of the converting charity. Professional advice should be taken.

CIOs: Northern Ireland

CIOs are not yet available for registration in Northern Ireland. In due course, requirements for their constitutions will be set out in regulations.

3 Governance and management

Meaning of governance

Governance is the means by which a charity is directed and controlled by its governing body (i.e. its board of trustees). It seeks to 'add long-term value' to the organisation; in a charity, this is generally about improving the quality of the charitable outcomes for the specific beneficiaries and the wider community.

The key aspects of governance are:
- providing direction;
- enhancing effectiveness; and
- ensuring accountability.

The charity's governance systems and procedures need to focus on these key aspects.

Governance is not the same as the day-to-day management or the practical operation of the organisation. It is at a higher, more strategic or 'bigger picture' level, creating a vision that helps the charity deliver real and lasting social impact.

Good governance is not an end in itself; rather it is a means towards ensuring the organisation's well-being and success.

Governance role of the board

The fundamental role of the board is to be the charity's governing body, providing strong strategic leadership and clear direction to the charity. The trustees should seek to do so in accordance with good governance practices and principles.

Systems and processes are important, but truly good governance has to be lived. Every trustee needs to embrace its values and collectively the board needs to encourage a culture of good governance throughout the organisation.

Independence in governance

It is vital that the trustees maintain independence in governing the charity and making decisions about its management. They must ensure they do not allow themselves to be unduly influenced by any third parties, including funders, donors or even beneficiaries or their families.

Trustees do not act as representatives of the charity's members or of any organisation that may have directly appointed them to the board.

It is essential that the trustees have appropriate awareness of potential conflicts of interest and conflicts of loyalty, and of the need to identify and actively manage such conflicts. See further comments in Chapter Six.

Charity Governance Code

The Charity Governance Code (formerly called Good Governance – A Code for the Voluntary and Community Sector) is a voluntary code intended to promote good governance in charities. Charities may use the code in whatever ways they find helpful.

The code is not a substitute for the existing constitution of a charity and each charity must obey its own constitution.

The code sets out a 'foundation principle' that all trustees:

- are committed to their charity's cause and want to provide leadership and help the charity deliver its purposes most effectively for the public benefit; and
- understand their roles and legal responsibilities;
- are committed to good governance and want to contribute to their charity's continued improvement; and
- are prepared to challenge, and be challenged, in a constructive way.

This foundation principle is supported by a number of further principles, with recommended practices in areas such as clarity about the organisation's purposes and the effective and sustainable delivery of those purposes, leadership, integrity, decision making, risk management and controls, board effectiveness and diversity, openness and accountability.

The code recognises that practices and procedures in support of the principles need to vary from charity to charity depending on circumstances, size, the charity's particular legal form and a range of other factors. It includes 'lighter touch' approaches for smaller charities.

Larger charities are expected to meet the spirit of the code by either applying its recommended practice or, in areas where they choose not do so, explaining what aspects of their governance they carry out in a different way.

The code can be used in a range of ways to assist charities in their governance. For example, it can be of particular help in planning and delivering induction for new trustees or development training for the board as a whole, and as a yardstick of good practice when reviewing and altering the organisation's current governance structures and procedures. Using the code as a tool for continuous improvement is strongly encouraged.

The code is written by a steering group on behalf of a number of partner organisations – the Association of Chief Executives of Voluntary Organisations, ICSA: The Governance Institute, the National Council for Voluntary Organisations, the Association of Chairs, the Small Charities Coalition and the Wales Council for Voluntary Action, and is supported by the Charity Commission. Copies are available on the code's website: www.governancecode.org.

Effectiveness in governance: some other reference points

Besides the code discussed above, charities can find useful reference points on good governance standards and principles in the following guidance notes from the charity regulators:

- The Essential Trustee;
- The Hallmarks of an Effective Charity;
- Managing Charity Assets and Resources: An Overview for Trustees (see the Charity Commission website); and
- Guidance and Good Practice for Charity Trustees (see the OSCR website).

Charity trustees: legal definition

The legal definition of charity trustees is the people who have the general control of the management and administration of a charity (section 177 of the Charities Act 2011 and section 106 of the Charities and Trustee Investment (Scotland) Act 2005).

Charity trustees: general legal duties

The general legal duties of charity trustees arise from common law (there is no specific list of general duties in the Charities Act).

These general duties can be described in various different ways. This is a summary of the descriptions in the Charity Commission guidance 'The Essential Trustee: What You Need to Know, What You Need to Do' [CC3]:

- To carry out the charity's purposes for the public benefit.
- To ensure the charity complies with its governing document (i.e. constitution) and with the law.
- To act in what they honestly believe to be the charity's best interests.
- To manage the charity's resources responsibly.
- To act with reasonable care and skill.
- To ensure the charity is accountable.

Some further specific duties apply to the trustees of particular legal forms of charity, in particular:

- the trustees of a charitable company have the duties of company directors;
- the trustees of a CIO have a specific duty to further the CIO's charitable purposes; and
- a CIO trustee with special knowledge or experience, or a CIO trustee acting in the course of a profession or business, is subject to higher standards in the performance of their general trustees duties (see section 221(2) of the Charities Act 2011).

Role of trustees

The Charity Commission summarises the trustees' role as the governing body of the charity in this way:

> Trustees have independent control over, and legal responsibility for, a charity's management and administration. They play a very important role, almost always unpaid, in a sector that contributes significantly to the character and wellbeing of the country.
>
> (Charity Commission, 'The Essential Trustee')

The OSCR comments:

> Charity trustees are the people who have general control and management of the charity and are responsible for making sure that the charity works to achieve its charitable purposes (the reasons the charity exists)
>
> (OSCR, Guidance and Good Practice for Charity Trustees)

In providing strategic leadership, the trustees should address finance, operations and the effective governance of the charity.

There are both collective and individual dimensions to the role. Each trustee must apply their own minds and skills to their charity and its affairs, acting selflessly in the charity's best interests. The board collectively governs the charity and makes major decisions about its direction, strategy and policies.

All trustees should contribute to honest and open debate at board meetings and, after appropriate discussion, decisions will be reached by agreement (i.e. trustees will pass resolutions). There may be a unanimous consensus, where all trustees agree with a proposal. Where views diverge, a vote will be taken and the decision will be carried, provided there is a majority vote in favour of the relevant proposal. Once a decision has been reached, all trustees are bound by it and they should do their best to ensure that it is carried into effect.

Key responsibilities of trustees

Trustees have ultimate responsibility for the charity and its affairs. Key areas for trustees to focus on include strategic leadership, financial management, security and correct use of funds and assets, pursuit of the charitable purposes and delivery of public benefit.

In summary, the key responsibilities of the trustees include:

- governance (acting as the governing body of the charity);
- strategic direction of the charity;
- safeguarding and correct application of all the charity's resources (to its charitable purposes);
- financial management, financial health, sustainability and solvency of the charity;
- ensuring the charity pursues its own charitable purposes and delivers the charitable public benefit for which it is established;
- ensuring the charity operates within its own constitution;
- ensuring the charity acts lawfully and deals with its regulatory and public accountability obligations; and
- identifying, and managing in an appropriate way, potential conflicts of interest (including conflicts of loyalty).

Above all, the trustees must act at all times in what they honestly believe to be the charity's best interests.

In discharging their responsibilities, the trustees must to some extent balance the needs of current actual and potential beneficiaries with the foreseeable needs of future beneficiaries in years to come.

Trustees' duties: Scotland

The general duties of charity trustees under Scots law are statutory (see section 66(1) of the Charities and Trustee Investment (Scotland) Act 2005). The relevant provision requires a charity trustee to act in the interests of the charity and, in particular, to:

- seek, in good faith, to ensure the charity acts in a manner which is consistent with its purposes; and
- act with the care and diligence that it is reasonable to expect of a person who is managing the affairs of another person.

Directors' duties: charitable companies

The trustees of charitable companies have the usual general duties of company directors, in addition to their duties as charity trustees. In practice these do not impose any additional burdens on the trustees, as they express general principles of behaviour that would inevitably be expected of charity trustees.

The general duties of directors (as modified by the Companies Act 2006 for the trustees of charitable companies, see sections 171–177) are to:

- act within the constitution and to exercise their powers for the purposes for which they were conferred;
- promote the success of the company in achieving its charitable purposes;
- exercise independent judgement;
- exercise reasonable skill, care and diligence;
- avoid conflicts of interest;
- not accept benefits from third parties; and
- declare direct and indirect personal interests in proposed transactions or arrangements.

Much of this amounts to common sense and points out what should be both obvious and second nature in any charity, which exists for the wider good of society, not the financial or personal interests of its trustees or its members.

There are also some specific duties under the Companies Act 2006 and associated regulations, which largely relate to public accountability and filing required documents at Companies House. These filing obligations are not difficult to deal with in practice, as most of the required items can be filed quickly and easily online, via the Companies House website.

Liabilities for breach of duties

Breaches of duty are a serious matter with potential personal liability for the trustees. The exact consequences of a breach depend on the relevant duty and the particular circumstances, but may involve:

- accounting to the charity for improper payments or the value of improper benefits received by the trustee or connected persons;
- compensating the charity for losses it has incurred as a consequence of the breach of duty; and
- restoring property to the charity.

Where a contract has been entered into in improper circumstances, it may be void and/or unenforceable by or for the benefit of the relevant trustee and connected persons (although the law protects the interests of bona fide third parties who have acted honestly).

Other liabilities of trustees

Besides potential liabilities for breaches of duty, trustees can be liable to some criminal penalties for significant failures in compliance with charity law, particularly public accounting and reporting obligations.

The trustees of unincorporated charities are not protected by limited liability, so they face risks of personal liability in the day-to-day management of the charity. The risks are particularly significant if the charity's assets are insufficient to meet a claim that arises against the trustees in relation to their actions on the charity's behalf.

Managing risks for trustees

It is important to keep matters in perspective. Trustees who pay proper attention to their charity's affairs and act honestly are unlikely to encounter significant problems. Any risk of personal liability for misbehaviour or substantial failures is small.

Liability risks in the charity's everyday operations are a different matter and should be distinguished clearly from risks relating to significantly inadequate, or wantonly wrongful, behaviour by trustees.

In a limited liability charity, the trustees are protected from personal risk in the everyday operations by the charity's independent legal identity and the limited liability protection it gives them. The position is completely different for trustees of unincorporated charities, without independent legal capacity. These charities do not provide limited liability protection and their trustees are exposed to personal liability risks in the ordinary activities of the charity. This is a cause of concern for trustees of such charities (e.g. trusts and unincorporated members' associations) – though many are surprisingly unaware of the situation.

Although trustees' indemnity insurance, funded by the charity, can potentially be obtained (subject to applicable statutory conditions and provided the charity's own constitution does not specifically prohibit this), it provides limited cover in quite restricted circumstances and successful claims are rare. See further comment on trustees' indemnity insurance in Chapter Seven.

Appointment of trustees

Trustees are appointed in accordance with the procedures set out in the charity's constitution. In a trust, the decision is usually a matter for the current trustees (though sometimes the founder or a third party may have rights to appoint some of the trustees). In a membership charity, the members may have the right to appoint some or all of the trustees. The board itself may also have appointment rights, but this may be limited to filling vacancies on a temporary basis until the next annual general meeting of the members.

Terms of office and cessation of office

There may be limited terms of office, specified in the charity's constitution. Although this is not a legal requirement it is regarded as a matter of good practice. Charities are increasingly encouraged to consider altering their constitutions to include limited terms of office, if they do not yet contain such provisions.

Trustees cease to hold office:

- at the end of a fixed term (reappointment to a further term may be permitted by the particular charity's constitution; there may also be a limit on the total number of terms that can be served);
- by voluntary resignation (it is both good practice and wise to provide a written resignation, which should be signed and dated);
- if they are disqualified by a provision in the constitution (for example, some charities provide a process for removing non-attenders after a certain number of board meetings have been missed without appropriate reasons);
- if they are removed under a specific power of removal in the constitution;
- in a charitable company, if they are removed by resolution of the members under the Companies Act 2006 power for members to remove directors from office (special procedures must be followed);
- if they are disqualified by law from acting as a charity trustee;
- if they are disqualified by order of the Charity Commission, using its discretionary power to disqualify trustees considered unfit (see additional details in Chapter One); or
- on death.

Changes among the trustees: records and notifications

It is good practice to notify the relevant charity regulator(s) as changes occur among the trustees (appointments or cessations of office).

Such changes must be recorded as part of the annual reporting by the charity.

A charitable company must notify Companies House of changes among its trustee board and of changes to the statutory details of any trustee (e.g. a change of address). There is a 14-day time limit. The notification can be made online, via the Companies House website.

A CIO must notify the Charity Commission of changes among its trustees and of changes to their details.

Details of changes must be recorded in the register of trustees for a charitable company, CIO or SCIO.

Decisions about trustee appointments and records of resignations or other reasons for cessation of office should also be made in the minutes of relevant meetings.

Disqualification of trustees

There are various legal grounds for the disqualification of individuals from acting as charity trustees or being involved in the management of charities. They include convictions for criminal offences of dishonesty, personal bankruptcy, disqualification as a company director, persistent breaches of public accounting and reporting obligations and wrongful or fraudulent trading prior to the insolvency of a company. In some circumstances the disqualification is automatic (e.g. when a bankruptcy order is made); in others, such as wrongful or fraudulent trading, a court order is needed to effect the disqualification. There is also a discretionary power for the Charity Commission to disqualify individuals it considers to be unfit to be a trustee (provided the Commission is satisfied that certain conditions are met). See Chapter One for further details on this power and the legal conditions that must be satisfied before it can be used by the Commission.

Officers: general

Most charities will appoint some officers, usually on an honorary (i.e. voluntary) basis. The most common officer posts are chairman, deputy or vice-chairman, treasurer, secretary or clerk.

While the holders of such offices may have particular responsibilities in the organisation, they should not act in general matters without due authority from the trustee board.

In Scotland, the term 'office bearers' rather than officers is normally used.

In a charitable company, an 'officer' for the purposes of the Companies Act 2006 and company law in general includes the trustees (who are the company directors of the charitable company). For some (but not all) purposes of the Companies Act, any secretary appointed by the company is also an officer.

In a membership charity, eligibility to serve as officers may be limited by the charity's constitution to those who are current members.

Any eligibility criteria and the mechanisms for appointing (by decision of the board) or electing (by decision of the members) people to the officer posts are usually specified in the charity's constitution. It may also address other matters such as the term of office, whether reappointment/

re-election to further terms is permitted and the general nature of the officer's responsibilities.

The detailed role and the particular responsibilities of each office will usually be dealt with in specific role descriptions authorised by the board. It is good practice to adopt such role descriptions (specimens can be found in the appendices). An officer's role description should be reviewed periodically and updated or adjusted if appropriate.

Chairman

Every board needs a chairman to oversee the functioning of the board and chair board meetings. The chairman must ensure the meetings are conducted in an orderly fashion, that all trustees have the opportunity to participate in the discussions and that the business of the meeting is properly dealt with. Typically the chairman of the board of trustees also chairs meetings of the members, in a membership charity.

The chairman is often appointed by the board from among the serving trustees, but in a membership charity the appointment of the chairman may be a matter for the members. The relevant procedures are usually set out in the charity's constitution.

The chairman's role in the conduct of board meetings is usually addressed in the constitution. The other responsibilities will vary from one charity to another. It is good practice for the board to authorise a role description for the chairman (a specimen can be found in the appendices). This should be consistent with the relevant provisions of the constitution. The role description should be reviewed periodically and updated or adjusted if appropriate.

Treasurer

If a charity has a treasurer, the post is usually appointed by the trustees. In a membership charity the appointment may be a matter for the members. The relevant procedures are usually set out in the charity's constitution.

The treasurer has oversight of the charity's finances and should take a lead on the strategic financial management. In smaller charities the treasurer may also be involved in day-to-day transactions and procedures. In a larger charity there may be finance staff to deal with those.

Collectively the trustees share overall responsibility for the financial health of the charity. They must take that responsibility seriously and give sufficient time and attention to the charity's finances. The treasurer should encourage them to do so.

It is good practice for the board to authorise a role description for the treasurer (a specimen can be found in the appendices). This should be consistent with the relevant provisions of the constitution. The role description should be reviewed periodically and updated or adjusted if appropriate.

Secretary or clerk

It remains common for a charity to have a secretary or equivalent role (e.g. clerk to the trustees in an unincorporated charitable trust). Private companies, including charitable companies, are no longer required to have a company secretary, as the position is optional. However, given the governance standards and accountability levels expected of charities, plus their substantial annual reporting and other public accountability obligations, it would be unwise for the board to dispense with the post.

Where a company's articles require the appointment of a secretary, that requirement must be met. For other charities, it is often a requirement of the constitution that there be a secretary or clerk (such a requirement must be met). The relevant procedures for the appointment of the secretary are usually set out in the charity's constitution.

A secretary may cease to hold office by voluntary resignation or at the end of a specific term of office, by removal from office (the board may have a removal power) or on death.

Charitable companies must keep records of the secretary in the register of secretaries and notify the Registrar of Companies of the appointment or cessation of office of a secretary.

In large organisations, the secretary or clerk role may be a paid staff post. It is sometimes part of the job role of another post (e.g. finance director or administration manager), whereas other charities choose to add the role to the responsibilities of their Chief Executive. In medium-sized and smaller organisations, it is much more likely to be a volunteer role.

It is best for the secretary or clerk role to be undertaken as a dedicated stand-alone function, if possible, rather than added on to another role.

The secretary's role should certainly be allocated to someone with sufficient expertise, knowledge and time to do justice to what are important responsibilities.

The overall purpose of a secretary or clerk post is to facilitate the good governance of the charity, assist its compliance with all applicable regulatory regimes, oversee its public accountability obligations and provide appropriate support to the board. The exact duties and functions will, however, vary considerably from one organisation to another, because of the diversity in purposes, activities, size and the legal form of individual charities. Besides having oversight of the governance systems, the secretary's or clerk's responsibilities will often also include internal administration.

The likely core duties and the common associated duties of a secretary or clerk are as follows:

- Ensure board meeting papers are prepared and provided to trustees prior to the meeting.
- Issue notices, agenda and papers for meetings.
- Attend trustee and general meetings.
- Take minutes at board meetings and meetings of the members (or arrange for someone else to do so).
- Retain custody of minute books and other key records.
- Act as correspondent for the board.
- Make entries in and retain custody of registers.
- Oversee statutory compliance with regulatory and public accountability obligations (e.g. notifications to Companies House, the Charity Commission and/or the OSCR and other relevant regulators).
- Retain custody of the seal and supervision of its use (if the organisation has a seal).
- Act as custodian of the governing document (i.e. retaining custody of the physical item but also ensuring the terms of the governing document are known, understood and followed, as well as periodically arranging review and updating of that document).
- Common associated duties include:
- advising on governance matters;
- legal advice (providing and/or obtaining);
- providing trustee support, arranging trustee training and development (for the whole board), and induction for new trustees;
- dealing with property matters (including intellectual property);
- overseeing the charity's insurance arrangements;
- office and premises management;

- ensuring health and safety matters are properly addressed (the board must take ultimate responsibility, but may delegate some detailed matters to the secretary or clerk);
- dealing with data protection matters;
- supervising the HR functions;
- oversight of accounting and tax matters; and
- dealing with procedures for tendering, contracting and entering into other major legal agreements.

Secretary's liabilities

The secretary probably owes a common-law duty of care to the charity and should act in accordance with appropriate standards of behaviour.

The secretary of a charitable company is an 'officer' for most company law purposes and can potentially be liable for defaults committed by the company (for example, in relation to filing defaults). However, it is extremely rare for any action to be taken against a secretary.

If the secretary is also a trustee, the usual potential liabilities of trusteeship apply.

Meetings and decisions of trustees

Trustees hold formal board meetings in order to discharge their governance function and as one of the methods by which they fulfil their overall duties to the charity. Meetings enable trustees to discuss important matters and take major decisions. They also help the trustees to monitor functions and activities they have delegated to others (such as board sub-committees or staff).

The frequency of board meetings varies from one charity to another. In some charities the individual constitution will dictate the frequency of board meetings (though this limits flexibility and is not always helpful). Many charities set an annual calendar of board meetings, with the dates planned to ensure availability of all trustees (so far as possible) and availability of key data and monitoring information, such as management accounts and regular reports to the board from senior staff members.

The agenda and all the other papers for a board meeting should be sent to all the charity's trustees well in advance of the meeting, normally allowing a weekend to provide sufficient time for volunteer trustees to read them and prepare for the meeting. If the constitution provides a set period of notice for board meetings, that should be followed. Otherwise the board should agree a reasonable notice period for its meetings (seven days is probably about right as a minimum reasonable period of notice).

Declarations of personal interest should be made by trustees at the start of a board meeting, before any substantive discussions occur. It is good practice for the chairman of the meeting to remind the board members of the need to declare interests, and to ask if there are any declarations on the agenda items, as the meeting comes to order. Any declarations made require immediate attention in the context of potential conflicts of interest (see further comments on conflicts of interest in Chapter Six).

The procedures at trustees' meetings is largely governed by the charity's own constitution, which will specify the quorum required for the meeting to be valid, provide for the chairing of the meeting (usually by the chairman of the board of trustees) and may indicate voting procedures. Too much procedural detail in the constitution is undesirable; it should merely address major and fundamental matters, such as the required quorum. Where the board considers it necessary to document meeting procedures in more detail, this can be done in a board meetings procedures document, or standing orders, duly approved by the board.

Generally, meetings require the personal presence of trustees, gathered together in one place. However, electronic participation, at a distance, by one or two trustees who are unable to attend physically is possible provided the charity's constitution allows this. General legal principles suggest such participation should normally be by some form of audio-visual link, so all participants can both see and hear one another. Careful thought is needed to manage a meeting at which some participants are present through electronic communications (for example, in relation to the practicalities of voting by the 'distant' participants and in relation to security and confidentiality issues).

It is wise for the board to agree and document appropriate procedures in advance, if electronic participation is likely to be used by any trustees for some meetings. It is also important that all trustees do meet face to face from time to time, not least to build rapport among board members and strengthen the board's team-working capacity.

Each trustee has one vote on proposed decisions at board meetings and voting is normally by a show of hands, with decisions taken on a majority basis. If the chairman has a casting vote in the event of a tied vote, under the terms of the charity's constitution, the underlying principle is that this should be exercised to maintain the status quo, not used to force through a decision that does not command majority support.

Trustees' decisions (also known as resolutions of the trustees) should be recorded carefully in the minutes of the relevant board meeting. For the most important matters, the minutes will need to include some explanation of the background to and the reasons for the decision. This may be by means of cross-reference to reports and documents that were considered by the board before taking the decision. Where this occurs, a copy of the relevant item should be attached to or kept alongside the minutes, for future reference.

Any actions required in consequence of a decision of the board should also be noted in the minutes, ideally with a particular individual tasked to follow up to ensure the action is properly taken. The trustees should ensure there is appropriate reporting back to subsequent board meetings – not simply that the actions were indeed taken, but also about what the major outcomes of those actions were.

Written resolutions of trustees

Trustees may take formal decisions by means of a written resolution if the charity's constitution allows this. Usually the constitution will require signature of the resolution by every trustee, though it may provide for majority signatures to suffice. The full text of the proposed resolution must be provided to every trustee and sufficient time must be allowed for the trustees to consider whether they wish to sign the proposed resolution. It is sensible to indicate a deadline for return of the signed resolution, so the charity can be clear when (and if) a proposed written resolution is in fact passed.

Written resolutions can be a convenient mechanism for taking formal non-contentious decisions of an administrative nature, such as adding a newly appointed treasurer to the list of authorised bank signatories. However, they are not suitable for more substantive decisions, where full and frank discussion is needed before the board determines what it considers to be the right course of action on a particular matter for the charity.

Written resolutions are not a substitute for regular board meetings.

Records of meetings and decisions

A charity needs to make and keep records of all board meetings and all formal decisions of its trustees. A charitable company must ensure such records comply with the requirements of the Companies Act in relation to records of board meetings and, where applicable, records of written resolutions of directors (see section 248 of the Companies Act 2006).

Although minutes do not have to be printed in hard copy form, a signed paper copy does provide a significant level of legal assurance, as it is deemed to be a true record of the meeting and the decisions taken, unless evidence is produced to the contrary. It is not a legal requirement for the minutes to be approved by the trustees before signature but this is both usual and good practice. The chairman of the meeting, or the chairman of the next board meeting (if that is a different person), may sign the record copy of the minutes.

Delegation: general

The trustees of a charity may delegate particular functions and tasks to others and may authorise individuals who are not trustees to take certain actions on the charity's behalf. This is subject to the terms of the charity's constitution (e.g. in relation to the establishment of sub-committees of the board (sometimes simply termed 'committees')), the membership of those sub-committees, and the functions and powers they may be given.

Any delegation does not remove the collective and individual responsibilities of the trustees. The board retains overall responsibility for the charity and its affairs, and must supervise any group or individuals to whom they have given delegated authority, monitoring their activities with care. Regular reporting to the board and adequate provision of information to the trustees is essential as part of this monitoring process.

Sub-committees should have written terms of reference, approved by the board. If there are a number of sub-committees, it may be helpful to agree standing orders for general procedural matters, which apply to all the sub-committees, and specific terms of reference to provide the 'brief' for each particular sub-committee's functions. Particular care is needed regarding restrictions on any expenditure powers granted or any powers to bind the charity or commit it to legal agreements, including but not limited to contracts.

Trustees cannot delegate their trusteeship and the discharge of its responsibilities.

Delegation to staff and volunteers

A charity's staff members have delegated authority in the context of their employment, with specific duties according to their particular job role. This should be properly documented – in job descriptions, staff structure charts (to clarify reporting lines) and the charity's general employee policies and procedures.

A clear distinction should be maintained between the operational and management roles of the various staff, including the senior management team, and the governance role of the trustees.

Monitoring and supervising the staff is an inherent part of the board's overall responsibilities for the strategic management of the charity. Appropriate performance management needs adequate attention; however, trustees should avoid unnecessary and unhelpful interference in the staff's routine activities and resist the temptation to 'micro-manage' the charity.

Open two-way communication between staff and trustees is essential for healthy relationships and the effective operation of the charity. The Chief Executive Officer plays a particularly key role in ensuring there are meaningful communications between the board and the charity's staff.

Many charities are heavily or entirely dependent on volunteers, and some will have no paid staff at all. The same general legal and governance principles apply to delegation to volunteers, save that they are not in an employment law-based relationship to the charity, of course. There are particular practical challenges in managing unpaid volunteers and supervising them satisfactorily, so trustees must be prepared to work hard at this, in the interests of the charity and its beneficiaries.

Delegation of discretionary investment powers

There are specific legal restrictions and requirements in relation to the delegation of discretionary investment powers by the trustees of unincorporated charities (under the Trustee Act 2000).

Scots law applies particular restrictions and requirements to such delegation for all charities (under the Charities and Trustee Investment (Scotland) Act 2005).

4   Members and membership matters

Membership charities

Many but not all legal forms of charities have a formal legal membership, with a group of members who play a different role to the role of the trustees. Membership exists because the particular legal form of the charity requires there to be members as well as trustees.

Membership charities include:

- unincorporated members' associations;
- charitable companies;
- charitable incorporated organisations (CIOs); and
- Scottish charitable incorporated organisations (SCIOs).

Members have some rights and they also have some responsibilities in relation to the charity.

Members do not 'own' the charity in the way that the shareholders of a commercial company own that company. Their membership is fundamentally about providing the charity with funding (through membership subscriptions) and practical support – for example, members are often active volunteers deeply committed to delivering the charity's charitable activities.

Unincorporated trusts are not membership charities; they simply have trustees, not members.

Matters reserved to the members

Certain decisions have to be referred to the members for a formal members' resolution; these decisions may not be taken by the trustees. These reserved matters are particular matters of such importance that the law and/or the charity's constitution require them to be addressed at membership level. They are usually matters that affect the very nature of the charity and its fundamental structure or existence – for example, decisions to change the charity's name, alter its constitution or dissolve the charity.

Which matters must be referred to the members of an unincorporated members' association largely depend on its own constitution. Typically they will include alterations to the constitution and dissolution. Appointment of new trustees may also be something the board itself is not empowered to deal with.

For CIOs, SCIOs and charitable companies, the matters reserved to the members are specified in relevant legislation – the Charities Act 2011, the Charities and Trustee Investment (Scotland) Act 2005 and the Companies Act 2006, respectively (supplemented by relevant regulations). Some checklists are set out below:

Matters specifically reserved to the members of CIOs and SCIOs by legislation

- Altering the constitution (including its charitable purposes)
- Deciding to transfer the organisation's undertaking to another CIO/SCIO
- Resolving to amalgamate with another CIO/SCIO
- Resolving to dissolve the organisation voluntarily.

Notes

1. The constitution may reserve other matters to the members.
2. CIOs may amalgamate with other CIOs, and SCIOs with other SCIOs, but they cannot amalgamate with other legal forms of charities.

Matters specifically reserved to the members of charitable companies by legislation

- Changing the company's name
- Altering the company's articles (including its charitable purposes)
- Agreeing to a variation of their membership rights (direct or indirect variation)
- Resolving to wind the company up voluntarily.

Notes

1. The articles may reserve additional matters to the members, for example, the appointment of all the trustees.
2. Subject to general charity and company law, charitable companies may amalgamate with other charities or transfer their undertakings to other charities (regardless of legal form).

3 Some types of restructuring may require a members' resolution (this is not an automatic statutory requirement but will depend on the particular circumstances).

Members' rights, duties and liabilities

The rights duties and potential liabilities of members flow from statute and common law and, to some extent, from the constitution of the individual charity. There are significant differences between the various legal forms of charities.

Membership and its rights are personal to the particular member; they cannot be transferred to another person.

Unincorporated members' associations

There must be at least two members of an unincorporated members' association, as its essential legal nature is the association of two or more individuals for a common purpose.

Members can be the same people as the trustees; however, there is usually a wider membership, beyond just the trustees.

Income from membership subscriptions is very important for many unincorporated members' associations and, usually, at least some of the members are also active volunteers for their charity.

These organisations are based in common law, not statute, so the members do not have specific statutory duties as members. However, they do have commitments and responsibilities to their charity which arise from its constitution (e.g. to pay the relevant annual membership subscription for their particular membership class).

There are few inherent legal rights for members of unincorporated members' associations. The rights of a member are therefore heavily dependent on the constitution of the particular charity. Many constitutions are poorly written, which can lead to doubts about who is or can become a member, uncertainty about the rights of the members, difficulties in the governance, management and operation of the charity, and even significant disputes among the members or between some of the members and the trustees.

The members of an unincorporated members' association do not have the protection of limited liability. The liability risks in the day-to-day activities of the charity are highest for those who serve as trustees, rather than those who are purely members. However, there is the possibility of liabilities extending to members and there is some doubt about the legal boundaries, especially if the association's assets prove to be inadequate to meet liabilities to third parties.

Charitable companies

The statutory minimum number of members for a private company is one, but the articles of a charitable company will usually require a minimum of at least three members.

Members can be the same people as the trustees, or there may be a wider membership, beyond just the trustees.

Income from membership subscriptions is very important for many charitable companies and, usually, at least some of the members are also active volunteers for their charity.

A member of a charitable company does not have specific statutory duties as a member. However, a member does have responsibilities to the charity which arise from the charity's articles (for example, to pay the relevant annual membership subscription for their particular membership class).

The members' role is mainly passive, in the context of the governance and management of a charitable company. In practice it is probably limited to voting at the AGM on candidates proposed for appointment as trustees.

The members of a charitable company do have significant statutory rights, arising from company law. These are in addition to their rights under the particular company's articles. The statutory rights include the right to:

- Attend, speak and vote at general meetings of the members (unless the particular membership class held has restrictions in these matters, imposed by the company's articles).
- Appoint a proxy of the member's choice to attend, speak and vote at any general meeting on the appointing member's behalf.
- Vote on written resolutions (provided the member is an 'eligible member' in relation to the particular resolution).
- Receive copies of the annual accounts and reports of the company.

Note that item 1 is subject to the specific rights of the individual class of membership held by the member in question. The articles should set out clearly any restrictions, for instance, that a particular class of members have restricted voting rights or no voting rights.

Unless the membership class held has no voting rights at all, a member can always exercise their statutory right to appoint a proxy. This right cannot be removed or restricted by any provisions in the company's articles (as was once the case under previous company law). Any clause that attempts to restrict the choice of proxy (e.g. that only another member of the company can be appointed) is ineffective. Such out-of-date provisions should be removed, by altering the articles, to avoid confusion and accidental infringement of members' rights.

Items 3 and 4 cannot be restricted or removed, by provisions in the articles, as they are absolute rights. Note that the members do not approve the annual accounts, that approval is the legal responsibility of the board of trustees.

Collectively, members also have particular rights in relation to matters reserved to the members, which the board cannot deal with. The Companies Act 2006 deliberately gives the members the power to make certain decisions, and important examples include the following:

- A special resolution of the members is required to alter the articles or change the company's name (in the latter case, unless the articles give a specific power to the directors to alter the name, which is rare).
- A director can be removed from office *as a director* by ordinary resolution of the members in general meeting (this cannot be done by written resolution).
- The auditor can be removed, by an ordinary resolution of the members in general meeting, before the end of their period of office.

Special notice must be given by the proposing member to the company of any proposed resolution to remove a director or the auditor and other detailed procedural requirements apply. The director or auditor has various rights, including the right to attend and speak at the relevant general meeting.

Forcible removal of a director is a serious and potentially risky matter, so appropriate legal advice should always be taken before embarking upon such a course of action.

The members of a charitable company have the protection of limited liability, through the legal mechanism of the guarantee. By becoming members they guarantee that they will contribute to the company's assets on winding-up at a fixed amount (typically just £1). The sum will not actually have to be paid unless and until the company enters insolvent liquidation. The guarantee level is fixed when the company is incorporated and cannot subsequently be increased. It is not possible to set different levels of guarantee for different membership classes.

CIOs

A CIO must have at least one member (usually there will be more). Members can be the same people as the trustees or there may be a wider membership, beyond just the trustees. Members may contribute to the CIO's funding through annual membership subscriptions. Some of the members may be active volunteers for the CIO.

A member of a CIO has a statutory duty to exercise powers of membership in a way that the member decides, in good faith, would be most likely to further the charitable purposes of the CIO (see section 220 of the Charities Act 2011). This is in addition to the member's responsibilities to the CIO which arise from its constitution (for example, to pay the relevant annual membership subscription for their particular membership class).

The members' role in a CIO is mainly passive in practice, in the context of its day-to-day governance and management. However, because of the statutory duty of CIO members, they do need to take an active interest in the CIO and think carefully about how they exercise their membership rights in relation to its governance. Members should therefore ensure they do attend the statutory members' meeting and vote on candidates proposed for appointment as trustees.

Members' rights in a CIO are broadly comparable to the rights of members in a charitable company. However, the statutory rights of a CIO's members are more limited – for instance, they do not have a statutory right to appoint proxies to attend members' meetings on their behalf and may only do so if the particular CIO's constitution provides for this.

Certain rights are common to the members of all CIOs as they flow from the Charities Act and the CIO regulations. Other rights depend on the particular CIO's constitution.

The members of a CIO have the protection of limited liability.

The members may or may not have a liability to contribute to the CIO's assets on winding-up. If they do have such a liability it will be of a fixed amount, specified in the CIO's constitution.

SCIOs

A SCIO must have at least two members. Members can be the same people as the trustees or there may be a wider membership, beyond just the trustees. Members may contribute to the SCIO's funding through annual membership subscriptions. Some of the members may be active volunteers for the SCIO.

A member of a SCIO has statutory duties to:

- act in the interests of the SCIO; and
- seek, in good faith, to ensure the SCIO acts in a manner that is consistent with its charitable purposes (see section 55 of the Charities and Trustee Investment (Scotland) Act 2005).

These duties are in addition to the member's responsibilities to the SCIO which arise from its constitution (e.g. to pay the relevant annual membership subscription for their particular membership class).

The members' role in a SCIO is mainly passive in practice, in the context of the day-to-day governance and management of the SCIO. However, because of the statutory duties of SCIO members, they do need to take an active interest in the SCIO and think carefully about how they exercise their membership rights in relation to its affairs in general and in particular when exercising their membership rights in relation to its governance. Members should therefore ensure they do attend the statutory members' meeting and vote on candidates proposed for appointment as trustees.

Members' rights in a SCIO are broadly comparable to the rights of members in a charitable company. However, the statutory rights of a SCIO's members are more limited – for instance, they do not have a statutory right to appoint proxies to attend members' meetings on their behalf and may only do so if the particular SCIO's constitution provides for this.

Certain rights are common to the members of all SCIOs as they flow from the Charities and Trustee Investment (Scotland) Act and the SCIO regulations. Other rights depend on the particular SCIO's constitution.

The members of a SCIO have the protection of limited liability.

The members may or may not have a liability to contribute to the SCIO's assets on winding-up. If they do have such a liability it will be of a fixed amount, specified in the SCIO's constitution.

Members' meetings and decisions

In most membership charities, formal meetings of the members will be held from time to time. This may occur because it is required by law (as is the case for SCIOs). Alternatively it may occur because the constitution demands it – for example, a requirement to hold an annual general meeting of the members. It may also occur because there is some particular decision to be taken, or authorisation needed, which either the law or the constitution requires to be dealt with by the members, not by the charity's trustees.

Examples of matters that are likely to need a members' decision or otherwise need the authority of the members are:

- a change to the charity's name;
- alteration of its constitution; or
- a decision to wind up a solvent charity (winding up of an insolvent organisation is more likely to be triggered by legal action taken by creditors or the exercise of other rights by creditors).

In charitable companies, CIOs and SCIOs relevant statutory provisions require certain decisions to be taken by the members (see the checklists of matters reserved to the members of CIOs, SCIOs and charitable companies earlier in this chapter).

Chairing and conduct of meetings

The constitution of a charity normally indicates who takes the chair at a general meeting of the members and provides some powers for the chairman of that meeting. Typically, the current chairman of the board is entitled to take the chair, if attending the meeting.

The essential role of the chairman at the meeting is to ensure it is conducted in an orderly fashion and that the business is properly dealt with. In addition to any specific provisions in the individual charity's constitution, there are general legal principles the chairman may use for guidance, such as the need to deal fairly with all members, ensuring their rights are respected and can be exercised effectively (e.g. the chairman must ensure that Companies Act 2006 rules relevant to general meetings of the members and members' resolutions are observed).

Quorum

The quorum is the minimum number of participants with voting rights who must be present before the meeting can validly conduct business. This is normally specified in the charity's constitution.

In a charitable company, if its articles fail to state a quorum (which is unlikely), the Companies Act 2006 default rule is two qualifying persons (see section 318). A 'qualifying person' is:

- an individual who is a member of the company;
- an authorised representative of a corporation that is a member; or
- a proxy for any member.

There is a special rule for single-member companies, which can have a valid quorum of one while they have just one member (regardless of their articles). A charitable company is unlikely to be a single-member company.

Proxies

Members of unincorporated members' associations, CIOs and SCIOs only have the right to appoint proxies if the particular charity's constitution permits them to do so. The constitution may impose restrictions such as limiting the choice of proxy to one of the other members.

A member of a charitable company has an absolute right to appoint a proxy to attend a meeting on their behalf. The proxy can be anyone of the member's choice, and may be instructed how to vote or authorised to make their own decision. The company's articles cannot override these rights (e.g. attempt to restrict the choice of proxy) and any attempt to do so is invalid.

Voting

Voting rights of the members of unincorporated members' associations, CIOs and SCIOs depend on the particular charity's constitution. The rights may vary between different classes of membership and there may be one or more membership classes that do not have voting rights (this is sometimes, though not always, the case for honorary members).

Members of charitable companies have the voting rights set out in the particular company's articles. The rights may vary between different classes of membership and again there may be one or more membership classes that do not have voting rights.

Corporate members of a charitable company can attend and vote at a general meeting of that company's members by appointing an authorised representative or a proxy. Following reforms introduced by the Companies Act 2006, there is little practical difference between these two options.

Generally, voting on a resolution is conducted by a show of hands. However, it can also be by poll (effectively a written ballot). For charitable companies, the Companies Act provides minimum rights for members to demand a poll. An individual company's articles may add to these (but cannot remove or limit them).

Conduct of meetings

Other rules regarding conduct of members' meetings are usually set out in the particular charity's constitution. For charitable companies, to the extent the articles are silent, there are default rules in the Companies Act 2006.

Members' meetings and decisions: unincorporated members' associations

Procedures and other requirements for members' meetings and decisions in an unincorporated organisation largely depend on its particular constitution. This is also true with regard to the members' rights at such a meeting. There may be some rules, bye-laws or standing orders to supplement the constitution and deal with some of the procedural details.

Members' meetings and decisions: charitable companies

The requirements for arranging and holding a valid meeting of the members of a charitable company are determined by the Companies Act 2006 and relevant regulations made under that Act. They are also subject to the company's own articles of association, in so far as the Companies Act allows the articles to supplement the company law rules or, in some instances, to depart from a company law default rule.

Some company law rules relevant to members' meetings are mandatory, overriding anything in the company's articles. Any contradictory provision in the articles is ineffective and must be ignored on these particular points – for example, the articles cannot inhibit members' legal rights to use proxies.

Formal members' decisions in charitable companies are known as resolutions of the members. Such decisions are normally taken at a general meeting of the members of the company.

Members' resolutions may be either ordinary resolutions or special resolutions. A simple majority is required for an ordinary resolution whereas a 75% majority is required for a special resolution.

The Companies Act 2006 specifies which type of resolution is required for most decisions of the members (it is usually a special resolution – for example, a special resolution is required to agree a proposed alteration to the company's name or change its articles). Otherwise, the type of resolution required for particular decisions may be specified in the particular company's articles (which cannot override Companies Act mandatory requirements for the type of resolution required for a particular matter). If neither the Act nor the articles require a particular type of resolution for the proposed decision, an ordinary resolution can be used.

A copy of a special resolution must be filed at Companies House within 15 days of the date on which it was passed by a company's members.

Members' written resolutions: charitable companies

The Companies Act 2006 provides a procedure that can be used to pass written resolutions of the members of a charitable company (see sections 288–300). If a resolution is passed in accordance with the statutory procedure, it will be valid and effective. However, note that a written resolution specifically cannot be used for the removal of a trustee or an auditor before their period of office has ended (section 288(2) of the Companies Act 2006).

Proposed written resolutions must be sent or submitted to every 'eligible member' – that is, each member entitled to vote on the resolution at the circulation date (which is the date the first member is contacted, if the copies are dispatched to different members at different times). The copies can be provided in hard copy form or by electronic communication (subject to the Companies Act's specific rules on such communication from a company to its members).

If the proposed written resolution is a special resolution, that fact must be clearly stated in the circulated resolution.

Any auditors in office have the right to receive all communications that members receive regarding written resolutions (section 502(1) of the Companies Act 2006).

The period allowed for indications of agreement to the resolution, by the required percentage of the eligible members, is 28 days, beginning with the circulation date (or an alternative period specified in the company's articles). If the necessary consents are not received within that period, the resolution will lapse.

A member can give consent by hard copy (e.g. by signing a copy of the resolution) or, provided the charitable company is willing to accept it, by electronic means. Note that electronic communications to a company by an individual member must comply with the requirements of Schedule 4 of the Companies Act 2006, whereas communications by a company (e.g. from a corporate members to the charitable company) must comply with the provisions of Schedule 5 of that Act, which are not identical. Both schedules apply regardless of anything in the company's articles.

The percentage consent required to pass a written resolution is:

- for an ordinary resolution, a simple majority of the total voting rights of the eligible members; and
- for a special resolution, a majority of not less than 75% of the total voting rights of the eligible members.

There are requirements to keep a record of written resolutions and the members' approval of them. These records must be retained for at least ten years. Where any such record is signed by a trustee or the secretary, it provides evidence of the passing of the resolution. The signature also means that it is deemed that the Companies Act's requirements with regard to the passing of written resolutions were complied with. (See sections 355 (1)(a) and (2) and 356 (2) and (3) of the Companies Act 2006.)

If a copy of the resolution would have to be filed with Companies House if it had been passed at a meeting, a copy will also have to be filed if the resolution is passed as a written resolution (e.g. if the written resolution was a special resolution of the members).

Members' meetings and decisions: CIOs and SCIOs

SCIOs must hold regular meetings of their members (at least every 15 months). This is a statutory requirement. The business of the meeting is not prescribed by law, although it may be specified in the individual charity's constitution. Otherwise the trustees must decide on the business to be proposed at the meeting. There is no comparable statutory obligation for CIOs.

Annual general meetings

A charity may be obliged to hold an annual general meeting of its members in each calendar year because of the terms of its constitution.

Annual general meetings: unincorporated members' associations

An unincorporated members' association must hold an AGM if its constitution obliges it to do so (there is no statutory requirement). The business to be dealt with at the meeting is likely to be specified in that constitution; if not, the trustees will decide what business to put on the agenda.

Annual general meetings: charitable companies

For charitable companies, there is no statutory requirement to hold an AGM. However, the articles of a particular charitable company may require the holding of an AGM and specify particular business to be dealt with at the meeting (such as the presentation of annual accounts and the appointment of trustees). If so, this requirement must be observed.

Annual general meetings: CIOs and SCIOs

SCIOs have a statutory obligation to hold periodic general meetings of their members (at least every 15 months). The business of this meeting is not specified by the relevant legislation, but may be specified in the constitution of a particular SCIO.

This is not strictly an obligation to hold an AGM every calendar year; however, a SCIO may find it convenient to deal with the obligation on a regular annual basis. If so, care must be taken to ensure there is no longer than a 15-month gap between one statutory meeting of the members and the next.

CIOs do not have a statutory obligation to hold regular meetings of their members. However, the Charity Commission's 'association' model constitution imposes a constitutional requirement to hold an annual general meeting of the CIO's members at least once every 15 months.

Annual general meeting business

The formal business of the AGM will normally be indicated in the charity's constitution. It may include appointment of officers, such as the chairman and treasurer and a secretary, if the organisation has chosen to have a secretary. In some (but by no means all) charities, some or all of the trustees may be appointed at the AGM. In some charities the board members are required to retire by rotation at the meeting; in others there will be fixed periods of office, ending at the AGM.

The formal business usually also includes presenting the annual accounts and trustees' report for the preceding financial year. It is good practice to allow members the opportunity to raise questions and make comments on the information contained in the accounts and report.

In an unincorporated members' association, the accounts usually need the formal approval of the members. The trustees must approve their own report, prior to presenting it to the meeting.

In a charitable company it is the legal responsibility of the trustees, as directors, to approve the accounts as well as their annual trustees' report (sections 414 and 419 of the Companies Act 2006). Likewise, in a CIO or SCIO, approval of the accounts and trustees' report is a matter for the trustees, not the members.

If the charity is subject to audit or independent examination require-ments for its accounts, these should be dealt with before the accounts are presented to the meeting. A copy of the audit report or the independent examiner's report will be included with the copies of the accounts sent out to the members prior to the meeting. This report is for information (the members are not required to approve it).

Where there is no need for any formal approval of the accounts by the members, there should not be any resolution to 'approve' the accounts and report at the meeting. Technically the members simply 'receive' these items.

In all charities it is appropriate that important aspects of the financial results, and the impact of key activities in the past year, are highlighted to the members at an annual general meeting. It is also important that the members have the chance to ask questions about the charity's activities, if they wish to do so.

Many charities also use the meeting as an opportunity to update members on progress in the current year and provide information to their members about significant future plans.

Membership: legal capacity and eligibility

There are certain underlying legal principles that affect basic legal capacity to be a member of a charity, especially where the charity is in the legal form of a company. Legal capacity is the key issue, and a 'person' in law has such capacity (unless and until that capacity is removed by operation of law or a specific legal order – instances of such removal of capacity by the law are rare).

Generally, a 'person' in law is an individual with full legal capacity, or an organisation that has its own recognised legal capacity distinct from the individuals who are part of that organisation (i.e. it has independent legal identity). Companies have this legal capacity and so do individuals if they are of adult age and nothing has removed their right and their ability to exercise control over their own affairs (such as certain mental health protective orders).

Organisations that do *not* have legal capacity, such as an unincorporated members' association, cannot strictly take membership of other organisations and so cannot become members of charities.

A charity may want to have unincorporated organisations in a membership relationship with the charity – for instance, if the charity is an umbrella or representative body for other charities, or provides coordination or support to smaller local organisations. The technical legal difficulty of lack of capacity for membership can be overcome through appropriate clauses in the charity's constitution. For example, such provisions could:

- allow relevant unincorporated organisations to nominate an adult individual to apply for membership of the charity (effectively acting on behalf of their organisation); or
- permit one of the current officers of specified organisations to apply for membership of the charity.

In order to determine who can apply to be a member of a charity, it is important to consider legal capacity (discussed above) and also to consider what eligibility criteria are specified under the general law or the terms of the particular charity's constitution.

Specific legal prohibitions are less likely to apply to potential members than they are to potential trustees.

Eligibility criteria arising from the charity's constitution are relatively common. Care should be taken to ensure that any applicant for membership does meet the particular criteria and suitable evidence should be obtained and checked before an application is approved.

The detail of the eligibility criteria will vary widely from one charity to another. In a charitable professional body, and in some specialist medical and scientific charities, detailed requirements regarding the skills, qualifications and professional standing of the applicant may apply. There may also be requirements for compliance with standards of conduct and adherence to relevant ethical and professional codes.

Charities with a wider public membership, beyond simply their trustees, may use quite simple eligibility criteria, based on the applicant's declared support for the particular charitable purposes, to encourage the greatest level of membership support from the public.

Membership: unincorporated members' associations

The members of an unincorporated members' association are those persons who have been admitted to membership in accordance with the eligibility criteria and admission procedures specified by the particular charity's constitution.

The original members are those who agreed to establish the charity and adopted its first constitution.

There is no statutory obligation to keep a register of the members, but it is obviously sensible to ensure there are adequate and accurate records of both past and present members.

Membership: charitable companies

The members of a charitable company are the persons listed in the company's register of members.

The initial members are the 'subscribers' who agree to become members on incorporation. These persons are listed in the memorandum provided to the Registrar of Companies as part of the incorporation process. They automatically become members when the certificate of incorporation is issued.

Neither the Registrar of Companies nor the relevant charity regulator(s) (the Charity Commission and/or the OSCR) need to be notified of subsequent changes among the members. However, changes must be recorded in the company's register of members.

Membership: CIOs and SCIOs

The members of a CIO or SCIO are those who are listed in the register of members. The initial members will be notified to the Charity Commission or the OSCR as the CIO or SCIO applies for registration. Subsequent changes among the members must be notified to the relevant charity regulator because the members have statutory duties.

CIOs and SCIOs must keep registers of members and changes among the membership must be recorded in these registers.

Admission of members

The process by which a person becomes a member of a charity depends on the wider law, the legal form of the particular charity and the charity's constitution.

Questions of legal capacity and the eligibility rules applicable in the particular charity, to members as a whole and to the particular membership class applied for always need to be considered before admitting a new member.

Some charities require an admission fee and/or a first year's annual subscription to be paid by an applicant for membership. Most require the applicant to complete a membership application form (this may be a hard copy or it may be available online via the charity's website). Formal approval of the application by the trustees may also be required.

For some legal forms of charities, membership is not formally achieved until the person has been registered as a member in the charity's register of members (e.g. this is the case for charitable companies).

CIOs, SCIOs and charitable companies are all obliged by law to keep a register of members.

Any other membership charity may have in its own constitution relevant obligations about the keeping of membership records.

Of course it is common sense that an accurate record of all members and all changes among the membership is a necessity for any membership charity (whether or not it is also a legal obligation for that charity).

Cessation of membership

Membership of a charity can end by choice, for example, by voluntary resignation. It can also end by 'operation of law' (as in the case of a member's death) or by some forcible termination of membership – perhaps at the end of a disciplinary process.

Forcible termination of membership

A member cannot be expelled unless the constitution empowers the trustees, or the members in general meeting, to decide to expel a member in particular circumstances.

The rules and procedures specified by the charity's constitution need to be considered and followed carefully when dealing with a proposed forcible termination of membership.

The rules of natural justice also need to be considered, so there should be a clear and fair process, involving the right for the member in question to know the basis for the proposed expulsion and to have the opportunity to present their case before any decision is made. It is not a strict legal requirement to have an appeal process, but it is good practice to do so.

Automatic termination of membership

Some charities' constitutions provide for automatic termination of membership in specified circumstances, such as non-payment of the required annual subscription for the class of membership held. This is different from, and must not be confused with, a power to forcibly remove a member by following a particular process.

Cessation of membership on death

Membership of a charity is personal to the individual member and ends by operation of law on the member's death.

Cessation of membership by resignation

Voluntary resignation is one of the commonest circumstances in which membership of a charity ceases. The constitution may include particular procedures that must be followed, such as a requirement for a written resignation and/or a particular period of notice of the proposed resignation date.

Membership records

All membership charities should keep accurate and up-to-date records of their members. Charitable companies, CIOs and SCIOs must keep a register of members that complies with the legal obligations for that register in that particular legal form of charity.

If the charity claims Gift Aid on donations from its members it must keep appropriate records to comply with the requirements of tax law and of HMRC. HMRC can, and does, carry out Gift Aid audits of charity records.

Membership classes and variation of members' rights

Some charities have different membership classes to which different membership rights and perhaps different non-statutory obligations of membership attach (e.g. different levels of annual membership fee).

Requirements and procedures for variation of members' rights in an unincorporated members' association will largely depend on the individual organisation's constitution.

In charitable companies, the variation of members' rights is subject to Companies Act requirements.

In CIOs and SCIOs, variation of members' rights is subject to the specific CIO and SCIO regulatory requirements.

In all charities, variation of the rights of one or more membership classes will require the approval of the members in general and, almost inevitably, some alterations to the charity's constitution.

Membership classes and variation of rights: unincorporated members' associations

In an unincorporated members' association, the particular rights of any membership classes will depend on the individual charity's constitution. The constitution will probably set out particular procedures for varying these rights, which may include obtaining a particular majority vote in favour of the changes, from the membership class affected and/or the membership as a whole.

Membership classes and variation of rights: charitable companies

When a charitable company has different classes of members, with different rights attaching to their membership class, the differences may be largely practical, such as different levels of membership subscriptions for retired members compared to working-age members. However, the differences may relate to fundamental matters of company membership, such as voting rights.

As a rule of thumb, a matter relevant to fundamental company law rights should be addressed in the articles (e.g. that a particular category of membership cannot vote at general meetings). Lower-level matters, such as differences in membership subscriptions, can be addressed in rules and bye-laws, outside the articles.

The variation of the rights of a class of members in a charitable company requires advance consent from each class affected (see section 631 of the Companies Act 2006). If the articles provide a variation method, that must be followed, otherwise class consents must be obtained either:

(a) in writing from the holders of at least three-quarters of the members in that class; or

(b) by a special resolution passed at a separate meeting of the membership class affected.

The courts have taken a wide view of what is a 'variation' of rights, whether it is a direct or indirect variation. In addition, the Companies Act 2006 specifically provides that any change to the articles with regard to variation of rights is itself a variation of class rights. It is advisable to take a cautious view and obtain consents if there is any possibility of a proposed matter being a variation of rights.

If the changes involve alteration of the company's articles, a special resolution of the membership as a whole is necessary to effect the alterations (in addition to the class consents). A copy of that resolution, together with the altered articles, must be filed at Companies House.

There are also requirements to file forms at Companies House when new membership classes are created, or the names of existing classes are altered, as well as when the rights of any existing membership class are changed.

Membership classes and variation of rights: CIOs and SCIOs

The particular rights of any membership classes in CIOs and SCIOs will depend on the individual charity's constitution. The constitution will probably set out particular procedures for varying these rights, which may include obtaining a particular majority vote in favour of the changes, from the membership class affected and/or the membership as a whole.

Informal 'membership'

Some charities have groups of people who are described as 'members' who are not in fact formal members in any legal sense. Rather, they are in some other less formal relationship with the charity, such as belonging to a supporters' group that provides volunteers or other practical support to the charity, or perhaps funding through regular donations.

Considerable practical difficulties and even legal risks can arise if charities fail to distinguish between their formal legal members and people in other categories (who may be called 'members' but in fact are not). The constitution should be carefully worded, to demonstrate the different categories and the different relationships they have with the charity.

It is best practice to avoid the word 'member' for any group of people who not intended to be formal legal members. Alternative terms such as 'supporter' are more appropriate. Clear and accurate record-keeping also helps avoid problems (including well-worded minutes recording admission of formal members and an accurate, up-to-date, members' register).

5   Public accountability and reporting

Public accountability

The public accountability of charities reflects the fact that they exist for the greater good of society as a whole. A charity exists to provide appropriate public benefit, through activities undertaken in pursuit of the charitable purposes set out in its constitution. It has funds and assets given to it (or otherwise acquired by it) that are held in order to pursue those purposes and provide that benefit. The law, therefore, imposes a wide range of controls and safeguards to ensure that is done properly. A major part of those controls and safeguards feature accountability in one or more forms.

Accountability is largely a public matter, requiring charities to make information available in a very public form. Oversight of this public reporting by charities, by one or more charity regulators, also helps ensure that the public's interests are protected.

An overriding aim of the public reporting requirements for charities is to ensure charitable assets are safeguarded and properly applied. The public availability of annual accounts and reports enables the public at large to see that this is the case.

Accountability of charities: the stakeholders

There are a number of potential stakeholders in relation to charity accountability. They include:
- the relevant charity regulator(s) and the courts;
- the general public, because all charities exist to provide public benefit;
- the charity's membership (in a membership charity); and
- current and future beneficiaries.

The concept of accountability to beneficiaries is easier to comprehend where the direct beneficiaries of the particular activities are human, whether people in general or a defined portion of the population. It is a little more difficult to grasp where the charity exists to benefit people indirectly – for example, through activities that protect and enhance the environment or provide for the care and welfare of animals or plants.

Accountability may also be due to other additional regulators, with regulatory responsibilities in relation to the particular charity because of its specific legal form or its particular activities. Examples include Companies House, the Care Quality Commission (for England and Wales) or Care Inspectorate (for Scotland) and the Homes and Communities Agency.

In England and Wales, 'exempt' charities are subject to regulatory oversight from an alternative principal regulator (not the Charity Commission) – for example, the Higher Education Funding Council for England (or HEFC for Wales) for many universities and colleges or the Department of Culture, Media and Sport for various national museums and galleries.

Accountability: trustees' responsibilities

The trustees must ensure the charity complies with its public accountability obligations. Charity law and regulations require the preparation and public filing of detailed information about charities, their trustees, their activities, circumstances, finances, funds and assets, and their strategies and plans – both current and future. This is addressed through:

- 'event'-related public filing obligations – certain events may need to be notified to the relevant charity regulator(s) (some changes also require the regulator's advance consent – for example, a change to the charitable purposes); and
- annual filing of accounts and the trustees' annual report and the charity annual return.

CIOs and SCIOs have particular obligations to notify the charity regulators of certain events (e.g. changes among their trustees) because of the CIO-specific and SCIO-specific regulations.

Charitable companies have obligations to notify specified events to Companies House because of obligations arising under company law.

Charitable companies, CIOs and SCIOs must also keep statutory registers. Most of these registers are open for public inspection (there are privacy protections for trustees' home addresses, and access to the register of members is partially restricted).

Trustees' annual report

With some exceptions for the smallest charities, the trustees must prepare an annual trustees' report to accompany the charity's annual accounts. The contents of this report are specified by the Statement of Recommended Practice (SORP), which sets out more substantial requirements for larger charities (with gross annual income over £500,000).

The largest charities (those subject to compulsory audit of their accounts) are also obliged to report further information on various aspects of their fundraising, in particular:

- the charity's approach to fundraising;
- its fundraising work with, and oversight of, any professional fundraisers/commercial participators;
- whether it has chosen to comply with any recognised standards;
- the charity's monitoring of fundraising done on its behalf;
- its approach to complaints about fundraising; and
- the protection of the public, including vulnerable people, from intrusive or persistent fundraising approaches and undue pressure to donate.

The trustees may add further material to their annual report if they wish (on any matters, not just fundraising).

There is no compulsory order for the required material, so the statement of the charity's purposes and the most important information – about the impact of its activities and the public benefit those activities have delivered – may appear before all the 'boring legal detail' of the required administrative information.

The SORP requirements recognise that numbers are not, of themselves, enough to show the overall picture of a charity's activities and its end-of-year position. The figures alone cannot tell the story of the public benefit that has been provided and the good that the charity is doing – an imaginative trustees' annual report certainly can.

The trustees are responsible for the contents of their annual trustees' report and its accuracy. The board as a whole must formally approve the report and authorise its signature by one trustee on behalf of the board.

Checklist of contents: trustees' annual report (England and Wales)

While the exact contents required in the trustees' report vary according the size of the charity, this checklist provides the broad framework of contents.

For larger charities note also the additional requirements discussed above.

Public benefit

A trustees' annual report must include:
  (a) a report of those activities undertaken by a charity to further its charitable purposes for the public benefit; and
  (b) confirmation by the charity trustees that, in administering the charity, they have paid due regard to published Charity Commission guidance on the public benefit requirement under section 17 of the Charities Act 2011.

Reference and administrative material about the charity, its trustees and advisers

This section must give the charity's full legal name (as on the relevant charity register) plus any other name by which it is known (i.e. any operational name) and the charity registration number. If the charity is registered in both England and Wales and Scotland (i.e. it is a 'cross-border' charity), the two numbers will be different (the Scottish charity number will be prefixed 'SC'). If the charity is in the legal form of a company, its company number must also be stated.

The address of the principal office must be given and, for a charitable company, the address of its registered office.

The names of all trustees must be stated, including all who served for any part of the year being reported on. If trustees have joined the board after that year but before the approval of the report, their names should also be given.

The name of the Chief Executive and the names of any staff to whom the trustees have delegated day-to-day management must be given (i.e. senior management staff).

Names and addresses of all relevant professional advisers must be stated (e.g. solicitors, bankers, auditors or independent examiners, investment advisers).

Structure, governance and management

This section must set out the legal form of the charity (trust, unincorporated members' association, charitable company, CIO, etc), specify the nature of the governing document and indicate the method(s) for appointment of trustees. There should be details of how new trustees are inducted, plus information about the general training and development of trustees.

The organisational structure must be described (e.g. committees and their roles, in the context of the governance role of the trustee board) and the decision-making processes should be explained.

If the charity is part of a wider network, information should be given about that.

Details of relationships with related parties must be given (the SORP defines 'related parties').

There must be a statement about risk management, including the review processes by which risks are identified, and the systems and procedures adopted by the board to manage those risks.

Charitable purposes, activities and achievements

This section should make clear the aims and objectives set by the charity, the strategies and activities undertaken to achieve those, and place matters in the context of the longer-term strategies and objectives that have been set.

The information must include a summary of the charitable purposes (as set out in the governing document) and a summary of the main activities and achievements of the charity during the year in relation to those purposes for the public benefit.

If the charity makes grants as a major activity, the grant-making policy must be stated.

If there are material social investment programmes and/or material use of volunteers, information must be provided about those areas.

Achievements and performance

This section must give information about the achievements of the charity (and any subsidiaries) during the year that is being reported. In particular it should review the charitable activities, explaining performance against objectives, give details of material fundraising activities, including performance achieved against objectives set, and commenting on material expenditure as well as projected future income.

Details of material investments and their performance against the investment objectives should be given.

Any factors outside the charity's control that are relevant to the achievement of its objectives should be commented upon. Those might include relationships with employees, service users, other beneficiaries and funders, and the charity's position in the wider community.

Financial review

A review of the charity's financial position is required (and that of any subsidiaries). The principal financial management policies adopted during the year should be stated.

The policy on financial reserves, the level of reserves held and why they are held must be indicated. If material sums have been designated for particular purposes, the amounts and reasons must be given, together with intended timing of future expenditure. If there is a deficit or surplus on the target reserves sum, this must be indicted, together with the steps being taken to address the difference.

Principal funding sources must be indicated.

Information about how expenditure during the year has supported the charity's key objectives must be included.

Where any fund is in deficit at the beginning of the financial year, particulars of the steps taken by the trustees to eliminate the deficit must be given.

For any year-end deficit, information must be given about how it arose and what steps are being taken to eliminate it.

Comparable information must be given in relation to deficits in any subsidiaries.

The nature of any uncertainties about the charity's ability to continue as a going concern must also be stated.

If there are material investments, the investment policy and its objectives (including any social, environmental or ethical considerations) should be indicated.

Plans for future periods

The charity's plans for future periods need to be explained, including key aims and objectives, and details of activities planned to support these.

Assets held for other charities

If the charity or its trustees hold any assets on behalf of other charities, a description of those assets must be given, together with particulars of any special arrangements made for the safe custody of those assets, and their segregation from the charity's own assets. A description of the charitable purposes of the other charity(ies) must also be given.

Annual accounting and reporting

Charities are subject to annual accounting and reporting obligations. The exact items that must be filed, the format and contents of those items, and the time limits for submitting them to the relevant charity regulator(s) vary according to:

- the legal form of the particular charity;
- whether it is registered as a charity on any of the charity registers in the UK (many charities in England and Wales are not required to register with the Charity Commission);
- whether it is subject to additional regulatory regimes and registrations (e.g. because it is a social landlord or registered care home); and
- the charity's income and other financial thresholds.

Reporting standards and SORP compliance

The SORP is the general standard for charities and specifies standards for annual accounting and reporting by charities, save for charities to which specialist sub-sector accounting and reporting requirements and standards apply.

Smaller charities are able to make use of certain relaxations, under a 'light touch' reporting regime. The charity regulators expect other charities to comply fully with the SORP standards in their accounting and reporting. Where there is any departure, the regulators expect that to be identified and explained.

Certain charities operating in specialist fields, such as higher education or social housing, are subject to special sub-sector version SORPs.

Other specialist charities are subject to accounting regulations specific to that particular type of charity (e.g. Church of England Parochial Church Councils and English Anglican cathedrals).

Accruals accounts or receipts and payments accounts

Whether the charity can prepare its accounts on a receipts and payments basis or is required to prepare accruals accounts depends on a combination of its legal form and/or financial thresholds (mainly income thresholds).

CIOs with a gross annual income over £250,000 a year must prepare accruals accounts. CIOs with lower income levels may prepare either receipts and payments accounts or accruals accounts. The accounts of a CIO must be filed with the Charity Commission (there are no exemption thresholds for CIOs).

SCIOs with a gross annual income over £250,000 a year must prepare accruals accounts. SCIOs with lower income levels may prepare either receipts and payments accounts or accruals accounts. The accounts of a SCIO must be filed with the OSCR.

Charitable companies must prepare accruals accounts.

Smaller unincorporated charities are usually able to prepare receipts and payments accounts unless their constitutions or a major funder require accruals accounts.

The rules on charity accounting are complex and the detailed requirements differ between the various jurisdictions of the UK. Specialist accounting advice should be obtained.

Approval and signature of accounts and reports

The trustees are principally responsible for ensuring annual accounts that comply with relevant reporting standards are prepared. They may engage professional accountants to assist and this is usually both sensible and necessary, as charity accounting and reporting obligations are complex.

If the charity is a trust, a charitable company, a CIO or a SCIO, the trustees must approve the completed accounts and their annual trustees' report. The trustees must also authorise one of the trustees to sign the accounts and report on behalf of the board.

If the charity is an unincorporated members' association, its constitution may require some form of approval of the accounts by the members. This does not remove the statutory responsibilities of the trustees to ensure the accounts are properly prepared and audited or independently examined. They must also prepare and approve their annual trustees' report before presenting it to the members of the charity.

Annual accounts filing at Companies House: charitable companies

In addition to submitting their annual accounts to the Charity Commission and/or the OSCR, a charitable company must file its annual accounts and trustees' annual report at Companies House. There are no exemptions for smaller charitable companies.

The time limit for filing the accounts and report is nine months from the financial year end. There are civil financial penalties for non-compliance. These are automatically levied by Companies House when the late delivery of the accounts occurs (no court action is necessary). In cases where there was also a failure to meet the deadline in a previous financial year, the second year penalty is doubled.

Table 2: Civil financial penalties – late filing of company accounts

How late received at Companies House	Penalty first year	Second successive year
Not more than one month	£150	£300
Over one month, not more than three	£375	£750
Over three months, not more than six	£750	£1,500
More than six months	£1,500	£3,000

Independent external scrutiny of annual accounts

The external scrutiny of annual accounts has largely been harmonised for all legal forms of charities in England and Wales.

For a charitable company, auditors must be appointed for each financial year unless the company is within a relevant audit exemption threshold and its trustees reasonably resolve that such appointment is not necessary on the ground that audited accounts are unlikely to be required (section 485 of the Companies Act 2006).

A charitable company that does fall within applicable audit exemption thresholds (gross annual income under £1 million), can have an independent examination on its accounts, instead of an audit. If its income is very small (under £25,000), no external scrutiny is obligatory under statutory provisions. In both cases, this is provided the company's articles do not impose an audit requirement.

The thresholds for charitable companies and unincorporated charities are shown in Table 4 below.

Table 3: External scrutiny requirements and exemption thresholds – charities in England and Wales

Statutory audit or other scrutiny report	Threshold	Type of accounts
None	Gross income ceiling £25,000	Receipts and payments option (but not for companies, which must prepare accruals accounts)
Report by an independent examiner**	Gross income ceiling £500,000	As above
Report by independent examiner.** Audit if value of gross assets over £3.26m (or audit required for some other reason)	Gross income ceiling £1 million	Accruals
Full statutory audit report: Charities Act (non-company charities) or Companies Act 2006 (companies)	Gross income above £1 million	Accruals

Notes

* The independent examiner must be suitably qualified, in accordance with relevant regulations, if the charity's gross income exceeded £250,000.

CIOs may choose to prepare their annual accounts on a receipts and payments basis if their income does not exceed £250,000. Above that threshold, a CIO must prepare accruals accounts.

Note that the statutory provisions regarding audit exemption and independent examination are permissive, not overriding. If the charity's constitution requires an audit, that requirement must be followed. In addition, some major funders (particularly public bodies) may require a charity to have its accounts audited.

While external scrutiny of annual accounts is important, trustees should never over-rely on it. They should recognise that there is no substitute for sound financial management and adequate internal controls on a day-to-day basis.

Independent scrutiny of annual accounts: Scotland and Northern Ireland

Different thresholds and exemption provisions apply to unincorporated charities under charity law in Scotland. There will be a statutory audit requirement if:

- the gross income for the year is £500,000 or more; or
- gross assets at the financial year end exceed £2.8 million and the charity has prepared accrued accounts.

Charitable companies are subject to the same thresholds as are applicable to charitable companies in England and Wales because company law has UK-wide application.

For Northern Ireland, charity accounting regulations require independent examination of accounts by a person with the requisite skills, if the annual income is up to £250,000. If the income is over £250,000 but not above £500,000, the examiner must be professionally qualified. For charities with income above £500,000 full audit is required.

Audit

An audit provides reasonable assurance that the accounts are free from material misstatement (whether caused by error, fraud or other irregularity). In carrying out an audit, the auditor is subject to professional and ethical auditing standards specified by both the UK's Audit and Assurance Council, and international audit authorities. Statutory audits can only be carried out by registered auditors. The auditor's report is addressed to the trustees but is a matter of public record and is attached to the publicly filed copy of the charity's accounts.

Independent examination

An independent examination is a form of external scrutiny of the annual accounts that is less rigorous than an audit. It offers an assurance that nothing has been found that needs to be brought to the attention of the trustees. The report is addressed to the trustees but is a matter of public record and is attached to the publicly filed copy of the charity's accounts.

Charity annual return

Charities in England and Wales must file a charity annual return unless they fall below the relevant thresholds. The return is filed with the appropriate charity regulator. The forms for each jurisdiction are different and are also subject to periodic changes.

A 'cross-border' charity, registered on the Scottish Charity Register as well as being registered with the Charity Commission in England and Wales, must file a charity annual return with the OSCR as well as with the Commission.

For charities in Northern Ireland, an annual monitoring return must be filed with the Charity Commission for Northern Ireland.

Charity annual return and annual accounts filing: England and Wales

Smaller registered charities (with an annual income under £10,000) that are not CIOs do not have to provide a charity annual return but must keep their public registered details up to date. This can be dealt with online via the Charity Commission's website.

However, all CIOs are obliged to file a charity annual return (regardless of their annual income level). CIOs are also obliged to file annual accounts, regardless of their income level.

Registered charities in other legal forms that have an annual income of £10,000 or more must file a charity annual return. This can be dealt with online via the Commission's website. The return provides information about income and expenditure, changes to the charity's contact details, changes among its trustees (including changes to their residential addresses, though that information will not be made public) and details of the charity's geographic area of operation.

For registered charities with an income between £25,000 and £500,000, the return must also confirm there are no serious incidents or other matters that should be reported to the Charity Commission. The annual accounts and trustees' annual report must be filed with the return.

For registered charities with an income between £500,000 and £1 million, a more detailed return is required, providing more information about the charity, its activities and its financial affairs. The annual accounts and trustees' annual report must be filed with the return.

Where the charity's accounts are subject to audit or independent examination, the relevant report from the auditor or independent examiner must be included with the accounts and trustees' annual report submitted to the Charity Commission.

The filing deadline for required items is ten months from the charity's financial year end.

Charitable companies must also file their annual accounts and trustees' annual report with Companies House within *nine* months of the financial year end (see further comments earlier in this chapter).

Charity annual return and annual accounts filing: Scotland

All charities on the Scottish Charity Register must file an annual return with the OSCR. This may be filed online via the OSCR's website. It must be accompanied by the charity's annual accounts and trustees' annual report.

There are no exemptions for smaller charities; every charity on the register must submit both an annual return and annual accounts to the OSCR (although the level of detail required in both is lower for smaller charities).

Charities with a gross income of £25,000 must give additional information on their annual return and those with income over £250,000 must provide the most detailed level of information.

The time limit for filing the annual return and accounts with the OSCR is *nine* months (note this is one month shorter than the time limit applicable for filing equivalent items with the Charity Commission in England and Wales).

Charity annual return and annual accounts filing: Northern Ireland

There are Northern Ireland-specific obligations for charities to file annual monitoring returns and accounts with the Charity Commission for Northern Ireland.

Accounting and reporting: the charity regulators

The charity regulators review the contents of a charity's annual accounts and reports as part of their monitoring of the charity. Particular scrutiny is given to areas such as:

- public benefit reporting;
- the proper pursuit of the charitable purposes;
- correct application of funds and assets;
- conflicts of interest;
- improper trading activities by the charity itself or improper dealings with a trading subsidiary; and
- improper payments to, benefits for or transactions with trustees and connected persons. The charity regulators monitor compliance with accounting and reporting requirements, and with applicable time limits for submission of the required items. They expect charities to meet their obligations and will take action when major non-compliance occurs.

It is clear from the charity's public entry on the register of charities whether or not it has filed required items within the applicable time limits. If the records show non-compliance with the accounting and reporting obligations, or show that items have been filed late, the charity's standing and reputation with its beneficiaries, donors, other funders, supporters and the general public may be damaged.

Trustees who persistently fail to meet their obligations in relation to charity accounting and reporting are likely to have penalty action taken against them personally and could, ultimately, be removed and disqualified from acting as charity trustees in the future.

Company confirmation statement (Companies House)

A charitable company must file a company 'confirmation statement' at Companies House every year. This replaces the old company annual return. The obligation is in addition to the obligation to file a charity annual return with the Charity Commission.

The confirmation statement must be made up to the confirmation date (a date not more than 12 months after the preceding confirmation date). If any of the information held by Companies House about that company has changed since the previous confirmation statement, notice of the change must be filed before or at the same time as, the confirmation statement.

A statement must be filed at least once a year. A company may choose to file a statement more regularly.

The statement must be filed within 14 days of the end of the relevant 'review period'. For a new company, that period is 12 months from its date of incorporation. For other companies it is 12 months beginning the day after the previous review period.

Electronic filing is easiest and incurs a significantly lower statutory fee than filing on paper (£13 compared to £40).

Public record and public availability of information

The relevant register of charities is available for public inspection in each of the UK's jurisdictions (England and Wales, Scotland and Northern Ireland). Each charity regulator's website provides open access to the register, with an entry for each registered charity.

Certain basic information is shown for every charity, such as its name, charity number, contact details and charitable purposes. It is also possible to ascertain the legal form of the charity (trust, charitable company, etc) as either this is specifically stated or, at the least, the type of constitution is stated. The type of constitution, taken together with any statutory ending to the charity's name, should clarify the legal form. For example, a charity stated to have a constitution and with the statutory ending 'CIO' to its name is a charitable incorporated organisation.

The regulators do not display exactly the same data on the charity registers that they maintain, nor is there a consistent presentation style between the three registers. Importantly, none of the regulators make the full constitution of a charity available online and currently only the Charity Commission makes full copies of the annual accounts available to download.

The OSCR sets out some 'headline' financial information, taken from the charity's annual accounts, but advises an interested member of the public to contact the charity directly if they wish to see a copy of the full accounts. If the charity has provided the OSCR with an electronic link to its accounts on the charity's website, that link is displayed.

It should be remembered that in England and Wales the register is not comprehensive, since many charities are not subject to compulsory registration requirements (approximately half of all charities). So the fact that an organisation is not on the register of charities maintained by the Charity Commission does not mean that organisation is not in fact a charity.

In Northern Ireland, the full register is being established, as the new charity registration and accountability regime is fully implemented.

Charities are obliged to provide copies of their annual accounts and trustees' reports to any member of the public who requests a copy.

Many charities choose to make their annual accounts and reports widely available, including on their own websites. This is good practice and demonstrates an open culture and wholehearted commitment to transparency.

Various other sources of information about charities is accessible to the public – for example, charities that have legal obligations to maintain registers (charitable companies, CIOs and SCIOs) must allow public access to at least some of those registers (see further comments in Chapter Seven).

The public record of a charitable company held by Companies House will include the company's articles (its constitution) and any changes to it that have been registered, as well as all annual accounts and trustees' reports filed to date.

6 Good stewardship: the correct application of funds and assets

Funds and assets: key principles

Charitable funds and assets are held by a charity in order to pursue that charity's charitable purposes for the public benefit. Effectively the charity and its trustees are custodians, or stewards, of the charity's entire resources, whether those are tangible (e.g. cash, equipment, land and buildings) or intangible (e.g. its legal rights in relation to copyrights and trademarks). This is the case whether those resources were purchased by the charity or were donated to it.

Funds and assets: trustees' responsibilities

Trustees are responsible for the care of the charity's funds and assets, and their correct application. In particular they must ensure the funds and assets are:

- safeguarded against accidental loss or deliberate misappropriation;
- applied within the charity's charitable purposes (and not beyond them); and
- used effectively and efficiently.

Correct application of funds and assets

The charity's resources must principally be used to carry out its purposes for the public benefit. In addition, funds can be spent on justifiable and necessary overheads and running costs.

The trustees must manage the charitable resources responsibly, honestly and reasonably. In doing so they must exercise sound judgement, making balanced and well-informed decisions.

In fulfilling their 'duty of prudence' the trustees should ensure the charity remains financially sound and that its assets, reputation and beneficiaries are not exposed to undue risk. It is important that the trustees also ensure they do not over commit the available resources or mis-apply any restricted funds and assets.

The charity's resources must not be used for any non-charitable purposes or even any charitable purposes that are outside the charity's own charitable purposes. Also, they must not be used for any other organisation's purposes or to provide private benefits or to further the interests of a commercial organisation.

Misuse of charitable funds and assets is likely to be a breach of trust. Trustees can be personally liable for a breach of trust, whatever legal form the charity takes. Insurance cannot protect against that, nor can limited liability status.

Safeguarding funds and assets

The charity's resources must be safeguarded against harm. Areas of particular importance to consider include:

- appropriate risk management;
- arranging suitable insurance cover;
- protecting resources from incorrect use; and
- protecting resources from fraud, theft and other forms of misappropriation or abuse.

Types of funds

Funds held by a charity, that are not subject to any special legal trusts that control how those funds are spent, may be applied for any activities that are within the charity's overall charitable purposes. These are known as 'unrestricted funds'. All charities need sufficient unrestricted funds to maintain their charitable activities, cover their running costs and maintain solvency.

A charity may also have some of these special types of funds, which are subject to additional restrictions on how they can be used:

- restricted funds;
- permanent endowment; and
- functional permanent endowment.

Restricted funds

Restricted funds are funds held by a charity for a specific, restricted purpose. Typically, the legal restrictions arise because the donor specified the restricted purpose when making the donation, or the funds were provided by grant for a specific purpose, or the charity appealed for funds for a specific project or activity. In older charities the restriction may relate to the particular legal conditions imposed when the charity was established or at the time it acquired a particular piece of property (this is relatively common in relation to some historic gifts of property for charitable purposes).

The restrictions must be carefully observed so that the funds and any assets purchased with those funds (or any specific asset that is itself directly subject to restrictions) are only applied for the specified purposes. A restricted fund should not be spent beyond the relevant restrictions nor on the charity's general running costs, nor should it be in deficit.

The charity must list restricted funds and assets clearly in its annual accounts, and provide details of the relevant restrictions.

If it becomes impossible to use a restricted fund within the terms of the restriction, the charity may seek the original donor's permission to redeploy the fund (effectively seeking release of the restrictions imposed by the donor). Where that is not possible, there may be other options for removal of the restrictions; however, these will be more complex and are likely to involve legal changes and prior Charity Commission consent.

Permanent endowment

A permanent endowment is capital funds that must be retained, to generate future income. Only the income (not the capital value) may be spent in pursuing the charity's charitable purposes. Generally, the assets that represent the capital can be changed from time to time (e.g. investments adjusted). Older unincorporated charitable trusts tend to have permanent endowment; it is less common for newer charities to have this.

There are legal mechanisms that can sometimes be used to remove or relax permanent endowment restrictions, subject to a range of restrictions and safeguards. Charity Commission consent may be required.

Functional permanent endowment

Functional permanent endowment, which is often in the form of land and buildings (sometimes called 'specie land') is capital that not only cannot be spent, but also must be used for particular limited purposes – for example, as a charitable almshouse. It is more common in older unincorporated charities, particularly religious, anti-poverty and educational charities.

It is difficult and often impossible to remove functional permanent endowment restrictions completely, though some relaxation may be possible – for instance, through an alteration to the charitable purposes and/or constitution of the relevant charity. Charity Commission consent is likely to be required.

Incorporated charities (such as charitable companies) cannot be the direct owners of functional permanent endowment. Where an unincorporated charity wishes to restructure, gifting its funds and assets to a new charitable company as successor to the old charity, special legal arrangements are required for any functional endowment. The old charity may need to be retained in order to hold the property in question, perhaps with the new charitable company as a corporate trustee of the old charity or as a managing trustee of the property.

Public benefit

The law requires charities to exist for the public benefit. In England and Wales the 'public benefit requirement' in the Charities Act 2011 requires all charitable purposes to be 'for the public benefit' in order to be charitable. This is effectively a purposes-based legal obligation, though it has fundamental legal and practical consequences for a charity's activities.

The Charities Act does not provide a specific definition of 'public benefit'; rather the law provides a range of principles, based on the decisions of the courts over more than 400 years, against which organisations are ultimately assessed by the Charity Commission and, if necessary, by the courts themselves. It is against that legal background that the Charity Commission issues its public benefit guidance, assesses new applicants for charity registration and monitors existing charities with regard to public benefit.

It is because of the public benefit requirement that charitable funds and assets are held, and why in practice they must be used actively to pursue the charity's purposes for the public benefit. The entire resources of the charity, and all its activities, should be clearly focused on delivering public benefit appropriate to that charity's charitable purposes. The main benefits should flow directly from the charity's activities, though indirect benefits may also contribute towards meeting the charity's public benefit obligations.

The type of benefit must be appropriate to the purposes and provided to the right beneficiaries, who may be a particular group (e.g. elderly people) or the public at large, depending on the wording of the individual charity's charitable purposes.

Charity Commission public benefit guidance

The Charity Commission has a statutory objective to promote awareness and understanding of the operation of the public benefit requirement, and it issues guidance on the public benefit requirement (which it is required to do under the Charities Act). That guidance is contained in three documents (available on the Commission's website):

- PB1 Public Benefit: The Public Benefit Requirement;
- PB2 Public Benefit: Running a Charity; and
- PB3 Public Benefit: Reporting.

In addition to that main guidance, the Commission also issues supplementary guidance, including:

- the Prevention or Relief of Poverty for the Public Benefit;
- the Advancement of Religion for the Public Benefit; and
- the Advancement of Education for the Public Benefit.

The Charity Commission regards public benefit as the core characteristic of all charities and suggests that its guidance indicates areas trustees should consider 'in order to show that their charity's aims (i.e. its charitable purposes) are for the public benefit'.

The trustees should consider the impact of the guidance on how they are currently using the charity's funds and assets, and how they plan to use them in the future.

The Charity Commission's public benefit guidance is reviewed and altered periodically. It is important to consider the current version, which is available on the Commission's website (www.charity-commission.gov.uk).

Public benefit – trustees' responsibilities

Fundamentally, charity trustees are required to address public benefit because their charity's charitable purposes are for the public benefit. In addition, they have specific legal duties to:

- 'have regard' to the statutory guidance on public benefit issued by the Charity Commission when exercising any powers or duties to which the guidance is relevant;
- report in their annual trustees' report on how the charity has furthered its aims (i.e. charitable purposes) for the public benefit; and
- state, in that annual report, whether they have considered the Charity Commission's guidance on public benefit.

There is no legal obligation to follow the Charity Commission's guidance on public benefit. However the regulator considers that in order to 'have regard' to its guidance, trustees must:

- be aware of the guidance;
- take the guidance into account when making any decision to which it is relevant; and
- have good reasons for making any decision to depart from the guidance.

Charity trustees should, therefore, always keep the guidance in mind when assessing the charity's current activities and planning future activities.

However, the Upper Tribunal (Charity) has reaffirmed that, within reasonable parameters, it is up to the trustees of a charity to make their own decisions about how best to provide public benefit. (See the judgment in HM Attorney General's Reference to the Tribunal – Reference the Independent Schools Council and others. The full judgment and a summary is available at: www.tribunals.gov.uk. In consequence of this decision, the Charity Commission reviewed and adjusted its public benefit guidance.)

Public benefit reporting

The charity reporting regulations and SORP require trustees to include in their annual trustees' report information about how the trustees have carried out their charity's purposes for the public benefit.

Charities with a gross annual income of below £100,000 should include:

- A brief summary setting out the main activities carried out by the charity to carry out its purposes for the public benefit.
- A statement as to whether they have complied with their duty to have regard to the Charity Commission's public benefit guidance when exercising any powers or duties to which the guidance is relevant.

Trustees of larger charities should:

- Provide a review of the significant activities undertaken by the charity to carry out its charitable purposes for the public benefit.
- Provide details of the charitable purposes and of the charity's strategic objectives.
- Provide details of strategies adopted and activities undertaken to achieve those purposes and objectives.

- Provide details of the achievements of the charity by reference to those purposes and objectives.
- Include a statement as to whether they have complied with their duty to have regard to the Charity Commission's public benefit guidance when exercising any powers or duties to which the guidance is relevant.

The report as a whole should speak clearly of the public benefit provided, since that is the raison d'être of the charity. Ideally, the good the organisation does, why that matters and how it helps both the particular beneficiary group and wider society (the impact of the charity's activities in pursuit of its charitable purposes) should shine through the entire report. Presenting this in a lively and engaging way, linking it clearly to the charity's charitable purposes, will help make the report more accessible to the general non-specialist reader (who may be a potential new supporter of the charity).

These public benefit reporting obligations apply to all registered charities.

Independent research, carried out on behalf of the Charity Commission, shows that compliance levels remain unacceptably low among charities in general and particularly in charities below the compulsory audit threshold. Even among those charities that do include comments on public benefit, few provide anything other than basic information. Many merely describe activities and how they were undertaken, failing to comment on the relationship of the activities to the purposes or to the charity's strategic priorities. Many also fail to comment on or evidence the impact of their activities in the context of their charitable purposes. There remains considerable scope for improvement.

Public benefit – Scotland

In Scotland, an organisation cannot meet the charity test, and so be registered as a charity with the OSCR, unless it has charitable purposes and 'it provides public benefit in Scotland or elsewhere' (section 7(1) of the Charities and Trustee Investment (Scotland) Act 2005). This is more an activities-based legal obligation.

In determining whether an organisation provides public benefit, the 2005 Act requires a comparison to be made between the benefit to the public and:

- benefits to the organisation's members or third parties (other than as members of the public) – i.e. private benefits; and
- any 'disbenefit' incurred or likely to be incurred by the public.

Where benefit is only provided to a section of the public and there are any conditions on obtaining the benefit (including any charge or fee), the 2005 Act requires consideration of whether the conditions are unduly restrictive.

The OSCR addresses these issues when considering new applicants for registration on the Scottish Charity Register and when reviewing existing charities to ensure they continue to meet the charity test.

Public benefit – Northern Ireland

Charity law in Northern Ireland has broadly comparable public benefit requirements to those applicable in England and Wales.

Public benefit guidance – Scotland and Northern Ireland

The OSCR has guidance on public benefit available on its website (see www.oscr.org.uk).

Under the law of Scotland, the legal requirement for public benefit is part of the charity test.

The Charity Commission for Northern Ireland has issued public benefit guidance relating to the relevant provisions of the Charities (Northern Ireland) Act 2008. It is available on the CCNI website.

Restrictions on private and commercial benefits

Charities must focus solely on the public benefit for which they were established; they cannot set out to provide private benefits. This includes benefits to individuals (i.e. benefits of a non-charitable nature) and commercial benefits to businesses.

Any private benefits arising from the charity's activities must be no more than necessary and incidental to the carrying out of those activities. For instance, it is acceptable that employed charity staff are paid appropriate salaries and that charities purchase office supplies or equipment from commercial businesses.

Trustees must be careful in this tricky area, especially when considering member benefits, donor benefits, commercial sponsorships and other fundraising ventures with businesses.

Restrictions on payment of, benefits for and transactions with trustees

Charities exist for the benefit of their beneficiaries and society as a whole; trusteeship is essentially a voluntary role, serving the community. Charitable funds and assets must be applied to pursue the charitable purposes and the charity must not allow its resources to be used for non-charitable activities. In addition, conflicts of interest must not be allowed to cause loss to the charity or to damage its reputation. These are key reasons why the law limits or prevents payment of trustees and the provision of benefits to trustees. Sometimes these rules are described as the 'no-benefits' rules.

The meaning of 'benefits' in this context is very wide, including direct and indirect payments, honoraria and other kinds of financial benefits, benefits in kind (e.g. free, or reduced-cost accommodation in property owned by the charity), commercial benefits to businesses with which trustees are connected, and payments and benefits to family members.

The law also restricts transactions between trustees (or individuals or organisations connected with trustees) and their charities. Sometimes these rules are described as the 'fair dealings obligations' or the 'clean hands requirements'.

Trustees may benefit from the charity's activities as general members of the community; however, this must not be on a preferential basis.

Payment of trustees for being trustees/employment of trustees

Trustees may not normally be paid for being trustees (nor should any trustee be employed by the charity to a job role). Some charities have a specific exception in their constitutions that may enable them to remunerate a limited number of trustees, subject to safeguards and conditions, or perhaps a particular exception allowing a specific employee to serve on the board of trustees (e.g. the head teacher of a charitable school). Such exceptions are rare.

The basic legal rule remains that trustees must act without remuneration or other financial or material reward, as the Charity Commission has commented: 'The principle of voluntary trusteeship remains central to the ethos of the charity sector.'

Note that repayment of genuine expenses, necessarily incurred by trustees in the discharge of their responsibilities, is not remuneration of trustees.

Remuneration of trustees for services other than trustee services

The Charities Act 2011 (sections 185–188) permits the possibility of remuneration of trustees, or 'connected persons', for the provision of services to the charity. Before pursuing any such arrangements, issues such as conflicts of interest and the risks to the charity's reputation should be carefully considered.

Strict conditions must be met before a charity can make use of the Charities Act procedures to purchase services from a trustee or a connected person. For example, the trustees must consider the guidance issued by the Charity Commission, there must be a written agreement setting out details (including the maximum level of the remuneration) and less than half the trustees must be capable of benefiting from the arrangements. There are also public disclosure requirements.

If the charity's constitution bans transactions with trustees, the constitution overrides these Charities Act provisions. Such constitutional prohibitions must be strictly observed.

Connected persons include:

- spouses or civil partners;
- parents and grandparents;
- children and grandchildren;
- brothers and sisters;
- spouses and civil partners of any of the relations listed above;
- business partners of any of the relations listed above; and
- institutions and corporate bodies controlled by trustees or any of the relations listed above.

These Charities Act provisions do not permit remuneration of trustees for being trustees.

Restrictions on transactions with trustees and connected persons

Charities must be careful about entering into transactions with trustees or individuals and organisations connected with them, as these often may not be lawful or proper. This is particularly because of the principle that private benefits should not arise from charities' activities and the principle that charitable funds and assets must not be applied beyond the charitable purposes of a charity. It is also because of conflicts of interest issues and because the individual charity's constitution is likely to ban, or at least substantially restrict, transactions with trustees and connected persons.

Where transactions with trustees or connected persons do occur, there are public disclosure obligations.

Directors' interests: charitable companies

Where the charity is in the legal form of a company limited by guarantee, additional Companies Act controls and requirements apply (because its trustees are also directors for the purposes of company law). These include:

- directors' duty to avoid conflicts of interest;
- directors' duty to declare an interest in a proposed transaction or arrangement; and
- directors' obligation to disclose an interest in an existing transaction or arrangement.

Directors' duty to avoid conflicts of interest (section 175 of the Companies Act 2006)

A company director must avoid a situation in which they have, or can have, a direct or indirect interest that conflicts, or possibly may conflict, with the interests of the company.

Directors' duty to declare an interest in a proposed transaction or arrangement (section 177 of the Companies Act 2006)

The directors' duty to declare an interest in a proposed transaction or arrangement has a very wide application. The duty arises if the director is in any way, directly or indirectly, interested in a proposed transaction or arrangement.

The disclosure must:

- be made before the company enters into the transaction or arrangement;
- be made to the other directors (i.e. to the full board, not a sub-committee);
- disclose the nature and extent of the interest; and

- be made for indirect, as well as direct, interests (e.g. the interests of family members).

If the original disclosure proves to be, or becomes, inaccurate or incomplete, a further declaration must be made.

Directors' obligation to disclose an interest in an existing transaction or arrangement (section 182 of the Companies Act 2006)

The directors' obligation to disclose an interest in an existing transaction or arrangement arises where a director is in any way, directly or indirectly, interested in a transaction or arrangement that has been entered into by the company.

The director must disclose any interest they are aware of and must declare the nature and extent of their interest. The disclosure must be to the board, not a sub-committee. A further disclosure is required if the original proves to be, or becomes, inaccurate or incomplete.

Remuneration of and transactions with trustees and connected persons – Scotland

Charity law in Scotland applies similar legal principles regarding dealings with trustees and connected persons as English law does. However, there are different specific statutory provisions regarding possible remuneration of and transactions with trustees and connected persons, set out in the Charities and Trustee Investment (Scotland) Act 2005 (sections 67 and 68). Subject to strict conditions and provided the charity's constitution does not specifically prohibit the arrangements, the Act's provisions can potentially permit remuneration of trustees and connected persons for:

- being a trustee of the charity;
- being employed by the charity; and
- providing services to the charity.

Remuneration of and transactions with trustees and connected persons – Northern Ireland

The Charities Act (Northern Ireland) 2008 provides a limited power to remunerate trustees and enter into transactions with trustees and connected persons (subject to conditions). Trustees are obliged to take account of guidance issued by the Charity Commission for Northern

Ireland. The regulator points out that this is a complex legal area and suggests trustees may need to seek specific legal advice.

Restrictions on benefits to members

The principle that private benefits should not arise from charities' activities and the need to ensure fair access to charitable services mean that charities must be careful about providing substantial benefits to their members. In addition, HMRC expects benefits provided to donors or people connected to donors to be limited within certain thresholds, so care must be taken to observe HMRC's guidance on this in the context of member benefits. Guidance is available at www.hmrc.gov.uk/charities.

Information provided to and communications with members, to give information about the charitable activities, is not considered as a benefit (e.g. annual reports, members' magazines and newsletters).

Members may receive the ordinary charitable benefits of the charity's activities, as general members of the community.

Conflicts of interest – general

Trustees have an overriding duty to act in what they honestly believe to be the best interests of their charity, at all times. They should take this duty very seriously and be diligent about avoiding potentially harmful conflicts of interest. They must not prefer their own personal interests, or the interests of any other individual or organisation, to the interests of the charity. In addition, the trustees must make independent decisions about the charity and its affairs – and be seen to do so.

Potential conflicts may arise in relation to contracts and many other types of transactions and arrangements. Besides such transactional conflicts, there can be conflicts of loyalty (e.g. if a trustee acts for two or more charities that may be in competition for funding or competing on tenders for commissioned services).

The interest that gives rise to the conflict may be a direct financial interest, but it may also be some other form of material interest. Indirect interests may also give rise to conflicts – for example, the interests of a trustee's employer, business or family members, or the interests of an organisation or body that appointed the trustee (such as a local authority).

Charity law in Scotland specifically provides that, in situations where there is a conflict of interest between the charity and a person responsible for the trustee's appointment, the trustee must:

- put the interests of the charity before those of that other person; and
- disclose the conflicting interest to the charity (unless some other legal duty prevents them from doing so) and refrain from participating in the deliberations and decision of the trustees on the matter.

(See section 66(1)(c) of the Charities and Trustee Investment (Scotland) Act 2005.)

While there is no directly comparable provision in the Charities Act, trustees of charities in England and Wales would be wise to follow the same pattern of behaviour.

In some charities, trustees will have inherent potential conflicts because they, or members of their family, are current or potential beneficiaries of the charity (for instance, the parent governors of a charitable school). Particular care is needed to deal properly and transparently with such situations, to protect the charity and its interests, and also to protect the relevant trustees and their reputations.

All trustees must act with clean hands, so any potentially conflicting interest should always be declared promptly to the trustee board (not simply to a sub-committee).

Usually the charity's constitution will set out specific restrictions and requirements relating to conflicts of interest. These are likely to include disclosure obligations and bans on the interested trustee being present while the board is considering the matter of interest to the trustee.

Candidates for appointment to the trustee board should be asked to provide a written declaration of interests, before appointment, so potential conflicts can be identified and addressed. It is also good practice to keep a register of all interests declared by trustees and to obtain an annual 'declaration of interest' update from all serving trustees.

At board meetings, it is good practice for the chairman to seek declarations of interest on any of the business on the agenda, as the meeting commences.

Conflicts of interest – Charity Commission guidance

The Charity Commission guidance Conflicts of Interest – A Guide for Charity Trustees CC29 defines a conflict of interest as:

> Any situation in which a trustee's personal interests or loyalties could, or could be seen to, prevent them from making a decision only in the best interests of the charity.

The guidance reminds trustees of their fundamental legal duty to act only in the best interests of their charity and states that trustees must not put themselves in any position where their duties as trustee may conflict with any personal interest they might have.

The guidance recommends that a 'three-step' approach is followed:

1 Identification of any possible conflict.

2 Elimination of any potential effect that conflict may have on decision-making (in serious conflict situations the Commission suggests the conflict must be entirely removed, not simply 'managed').

3. Recording of the conflict and how it was dealt with.

'Conflicts of interest affect charities of all types and sizes. They can lead to decisions that are not in the best interests of the charity and which are invalid or open to challenge. Conflicts of interest can also damage a charity's reputation or public trust and confidence in charities generally. These harmful effects can be prevented where individual trustees can identify conflicts of interest, and the trustee body can act to prevent them from affecting their decision making.

All trustees have a legal duty to act only in the best interests of their charity. The Charity Commission expects them to take appropriate steps in line with this guidance to ensure that they can do this.' [CC29]

Risk management

Ensuring that the major risks a charity faces are identified and managed is an important part of good stewardship. The focus should be on major risks, especially those that are more likely to occur in practice and to have a major detrimental impact on the organisation.

What risk controls are appropriate will depend on the size of the organisation, the nature of the major risks that have been identified and the range of activities being undertaken.

Particular risk areas to consider include:
- financial risks (including insolvency);
- fraud and other criminal risks;
- risk of accidental loss, damage or misapplication of charitable funds and assets;
- reputational risks;
- safeguarding risks (in relation to children, young people and other vulnerable individuals); and
- health and safety risks.

The board of trustees should take overall responsibility for the management of major risks, though if the charity is relatively large, some of the day-to-day risk management activity will be delegated to its paid staff.

The overall aim of a risk management strategy is to control risk and reduce the likelihood of serious harm occurring to the organisation, while maintaining its activities and their charitable impact. The strategy and the effectiveness of the charity's current risk management arrangements under that strategy should be reviewed regularly.

Land transactions

Ownership of, and transactions in relation to, land and buildings involve important and complex legal issues, and some potential liability risks for trustees. Appropriate professional advice should be obtained.

Incorporated charities can usually hold the title to land and buildings directly, in their own capacity. Unincorporated charities, which lack legal capacity, cannot do so. Instead, individual trustees acting as nominees (or some other custodian) must hold the title.

Trustees have significant responsibilities for the safeguarding and correct application of all the charity's resources. Particular care is necessary in relation to all major assets, including land and buildings, so decisions about major land transactions should be taken by the full trustee board (not delegated to a sub-committee).

The law places particular obligations on trustees in relation to:
- acquisition of land and buildings;
- disposal of land and buildings; and
- granting of security (i.e. mortgaging land and buildings as security for borrowing).

Few disposals of land require prior Charity Commission consent; however, disposals to trustees or connected persons or to charity employees certainly will do.

Some disposals are subject to lower levels of regulation – for example, a charity-to-charity disposal where the disposal is being made in order to pursue the disposing charity's charitable purposes. Likewise, a disposal by an unincorporated charity that is a mere technicality, necessary because of a change among the trustees, does not come within the general disposal rules in the Charities Act 2011.

However, unless one of these specific exceptions applies, a disposal of charity land to a third party is subject to compulsory requirements. For this purpose, 'disposal' includes a conveyance or transfer by way of sale and a lease of more than seven years. In summary, before making the disposal the trustees must:

- obtain and consider a written report from a qualified surveyor, addressing particular matters (such as price and disposal method – auction, private tender, etc);
- publicly advertise the proposed disposal (unless the surveyor advises this would not be in the charity's best interests); and
- satisfy themselves that the proposed disposal terms are the best that can reasonably be obtained for the charity.

Note that additional restrictions and legal requirements apply to land that is subject to endowment restrictions or other forms of special charitable trusts.

Land transactions: Scotland

Scotland has its own separate system of land law and land registration. The land registers are overseen by the government agency known as Registers of Scotland (see www.ros.gov.uk).

Where a charity is involved in any Scottish land transaction, it should seek advice from a suitably experienced Scots lawyer.

7   Operating the charity

Staff and volunteers

Every charity has at least some volunteers. Trustees are normally unpaid volunteers and many charities depend heavily or even exclusively on volunteers to carry out their work.

Larger charities have employees, with a paid Chief Executive (or equivalent role) and a management team working alongside other employed staff and volunteers. The management team are responsible for the day-to-day management of the charity, while the trustees are concerned with its governance and the provision of strategic leadership to the organisation.

Charities are subject to employment law just like any other employer. An employment relationship creates binding legal commitments on both sides and a charity's employees have the usual basic employment law rights, including:

- entitlement to holiday pay;
- the right to receive the statutory national minimum wage;
- the right to trade union membership;
- the right not be unfairly discriminated against (these protections are in the Equalities Act 2010); and
- the right not to be unfairly dismissed (this applies once the relevant qualifying period has been worked).

Other important legal obligations fall on an employer because of the workplace pensions auto-enrolment requirements, the legal limits on working hours, and the various family and parenting rights of employees.

It is important to distinguish clearly between the people who are volunteers and those who are employees of the charity. Ensure documentation is accurate in this respect and always avoid using employment terminology in relation to volunteers (e.g. avoid 'Volunteer *job* description' or 'Volunteer *contract*').

Employees' rights and pensions: charity restructures

Under the Transfer of Undertakings (Protection of Employment) (TUPE) Regulations, when an employee is transferred from one organisation to another, as part of a restructuring, the same rights and entitlements must attach to their employment with the new employer. This can be particularly important when charities take on former public assets or services (with their staff), when charities restructure or merge or when a charity moves staff between the charity and its trading subsidiary. Careful consideration of pension rights and any risks associated with potential deficits on a pension fund are important when considering any such changes or restructuring.

Employees: documentation and records

Employees are entitled to receive a written statement of the main terms and conditions of their employment. In addition, employers are obliged to keep various records relating to their employees, including national insurance and Pay As You Earn (PAYE) records.

Consultants and contractors

Charities sometimes engage independent consultants and contractors to provide services (e.g. fundraising consultants). The legal relationship is a contractual one, rather than one based on employment law. The terms of the contract should be clearly agreed and accurately documented.

Financial matters

Charities can only operate and make an impact if they have sufficient financial and other resources that are properly applied. It is essential that the trustees are wise stewards in this respect.

Financial management

Good financial management is essential to the effectiveness and the future survival of the charity. While the treasurer and the charity's paid finance staff will take the lead, financial management remains the overall responsibility of the trustee board, which should set key financial objectives, make the most important financial decisions and actively monitor the charity's financial affairs.

Collectively, the trustees share responsibility for:
- safeguarding and correctly applying the charity's funds and assets;
- ensuring funds are only spent on activities within the charity's charitable purposes and powers;

- applying restricted purpose funds only towards the relevant purposes;
- agreeing a suitable level of reserves and monitoring the actual level against the target;
- ensuring the charity keeps accurate internal financial records;
- complying with the charity's public accounting and reporting obligations; and
- maintaining solvency.

All trustees should take an active part in this and develop their skills in financial management. The charity should be prepared to assist such development – for example, by arranging training for its trustees.

Management accounts

Good-quality management accounts are an essential financial management tool. Generally, they are produced either monthly or quarterly. The management accounts should be more than a simple listing of income and expenditure, since the board needs to check that agreed priorities are being actively pursued and to understand the real cost of particular activities. It also needs to monitor performance against budget.

Financial controls

Good internal financial controls help ensure a charity's funds and assets are safeguarded and correctly applied. As part of the charity's wider control framework, they also assist the charity's risk management processes and help protect the charity against fraud, misapplication of funds and assets and accidental losses. Everyone in a charity should take the financial controls seriously and comply with them at all times. There should be a culture of adherence across the organisation and a willingness to follow good practice.

Segregation of duties is a key element of financial controls. No one person should have sole responsibility for the entirety of a transaction, nor should any one trustee (or employee or volunteer) have too influential a role in the day-to-day financial activities of the charity. For smaller charities this will be more difficult, as they will have fewer available people. A range of steps can be taken to address this issue, such as the board reviewing transaction reports or arranging periodic independent checks, undertaken by different people to those who are customarily involved in processing transactions.

Where there is delegation of particular financial activities and functions, to staff or volunteers, this should be clearly documented. The limits of each individual's authority need to be properly understood. The trustees should ensure there is regular reporting and that use of the delegated authority is monitored effectively.

Other areas of particular importance in financial controls include:

- custody of cash;
- processing, recording and application of funds from public collections, appeals and fundraising events;
- Gift Aid records and reclaims;
- banking transactions, including authorisation of cheques and other forms of funds transfers;
- authorisation of purchases and payments;
- payroll and other employee-related transactions;
- processing of expense claims.

The Charity Commission publishes a useful self-checklist on financial controls for charities (available on the Commission's website). Charities should also make good use of their external accountants and the charity's independent examiner or auditor in assessing the appropriate nature and the effectiveness of their financial controls.

Setting a budget and monitoring performance

The setting of an annual budget and regular monitoring of performance against budget are essential for an effective financial control system. That budget should be approved by the trustee board, prior to the commencement of a financial year. It should include realistic projections of income and expenditure in each main area of activity.

It is particularly important to ensure that any restricted funds are spent only on the correct restricted purposes, as specified by the donor or other funder.

Monitoring procedures should also focus on:

- reviewing actual income against projected income (both sources and amounts);
- checking actual expenditure against the agreed budget levels;
- monitoring bank balances and cash flow;
- monitoring the reserves level; and
- checking investment performance against agreed targets.

Financial records

Accurate financial information is essential for good decision-making and the effective operation of a charity. So the quality of the charity's financial records are crucial to managing cash flow, ensuring solvency, budgeting, monitoring expenditure and managing the charity's overall resources.

By law, charities must keep financial records which:

- record and explain all transactions, including receipts and expenditures, and the reasons for the transactions;
- disclose the charity's present financial position with reasonable accuracy; and
- enable the trustees to ensure the annual accounts meet the applicable financial reporting standards.

Internal accounting records should be kept for at least six years. Some of the records may need to be kept for longer, because of particular additional legal or regulatory requirements relevant to the specific charity.

Expenses

When carrying out activities on the charity's behalf, staff and volunteers sometimes have to incur personal expenses. Such 'out-of-pocket' expenses can be refunded to the individual by the charity, provided they were genuinely necessary and related specifically to undertaking authorised activities for the charity. Reimbursement of genuine and reasonable out-of-pocket expenses necessarily incurred by trustees in the proper discharge of their responsibilities is not remuneration of trustees.

Expenses of the charity itself should not be paid personally by individual trustees, other volunteers or staff then subsequently reclaimed. It is best practice for the organisation to deal directly with such payments.

The charity should adopt a formal written expenses policy, with clear parameters about what expenses can be refunded, in what circumstances and whether restrictions apply (for example, only standard class rail fares are permitted or hotel accommodation is capped at a certain level). This policy should apply to everyone who is potentially able to claim expenses (staff, trustees and other volunteers).

The charity should agree and document a procedure for expense claims, which should include these key features:

- completion of a standard expense claim form;
- provision of evidence of the reasons for expenditure and the amounts (including receipts);

- any mileage rate payable should be within the HMRC limits, so that tax and National Insurance will not become chargeable;
- the claimant should not be involved in checking and verifying the claim, nor should they authorise the payment;
- cash payments should be avoided, with BACS transfers or cheques used instead; and
- adequate records should be kept (to provide an audit trail).

Fraud, theft, bribery, terrorism and other criminal risks

Charities should be aware of the risks posed to them in relation to fraud, theft, bribery and certain other finance-related crimes, such as money laundering and terrorist abuse of charitable funds and assets. Such illegal activities can have seriously damaging impacts on both the finances and the reputation of a charity.

Good financial controls, diligent management and effective trustee oversight are all important tools in managing these risks. The greatest attention should focus on the areas of greatest risk. It is important to be alert and watchful, and to implement effective protective measures. This is an important part of the charity's overall risk management strategy.

Broadly, fraud includes intentional false representation, failure to declare information or abuse of position, carried out to make a gain from or cause a loss to another, or to expose another to a risk of loss. Charities are potentially at risk from both internal fraud, perpetrated by people within the charity, and external fraud, perpetrated by outsiders.

All charities should consider the guidance set out in 'Charity Fraud – A Guide for the Trustees and Managers of Charities' (produced by various public, law enforcement and charity sector organisations, and available at www.cfg.org.uk/resources/publications).

Other useful guidance is available from the:
- Charity Commission
- OSCR
- Charity Commission for Northern Ireland
- Charity Finance Group
- City of London Police
- Fraud Advisory Panel
- National Crime Agency
- Action Fraud (www.actionfraud.police.uk)
- Charities Against Fraud (www.charitiesagainstfraud.org.uk).

UK anti-bribery law places obligations on organisations to put procedures in place to prevent people engaging in bribery; failure to do this can incur criminal penalties.

An organisation, as well as an individual, can also be guilty of a criminal offence in relation to:

- bribery of a person;
- accepting bribes; and
- bribing a foreign official.

The offences are strict liability (no evidence of negligence is necessary) although if an organisation can show that it had adequate procedures in place to prevent bribery, there could be a successful defence.

The obligations to take preventative measures apply to trading subsidiaries of charities and probably to charity-owned community interest companies (CICs), where they are carrying out commercial activities in the UK or overseas. It is possible these obligations may also apply to charities themselves in some circumstances. In any event, it is clearly sensible to adopt anti-bribery measures to protect the charity and its reputation.

Money laundering is the process of converting the proceeds of crime into property or funds that appear to be legitimate and can then be used without arousing suspicion about their origin or legitimacy. Huge sums of 'dirty' money are turned into 'clean' funds through such processes. Charities can find themselves falling victim to this, when criminals use them as conduits for money laundering because of their inherent respectability and the levels of public trust and confidence that charities enjoy.

UK law makes it a criminal offence to carry out money laundering or assist a money launderer. It also requires suspicions of money laundering to be reported. The Charity Commission's guidance on 'Reporting Serious Incidents' provides details on how to make a report.

UK law includes a wide range of anti-terrorism measures, including investigatory powers for the police and security services. There are a number of criminal offences relating to terrorism, including financing or otherwise supporting terrorist activities and encouraging terrorism. In addition, there are various obligations to report suspicions of terrorist-related activities. Risks to charities in relation to such matters include:

- abuse and misappropriation of charitable funds;
- links to proscribed organisations that the Home Secretary considers to be involved in terrorist activities (charities must not assist or support such organisations);

- reporting obligations, where suspicions arise (these obligations apply to charity trustees); and
- reputational risks.

Charities should ensure appropriate protective measures are in place and followed in practice (such as regularly checking the list of proscribed organisations on the Home Office website). Note that appropriate due diligence procedures are particularly important in relation to:

- sending and receiving funds;
- appointing new trustees; and
- providing charitable services and any other form of aid or support, especially in high-risk territories.

Serious incident reporting

Where incidents of fraud or other financial crime are identified, or suspected, a charity should act immediately to minimise the risks of significant and irreversible loss or other harm. Consideration should always be given to:

- informing the police or other investigatory authorities (in some circumstances this is an absolute legal duty);
- making a serious incident report to the Charity Commission;
- disclosing the matter to other regulators; and
- notifying the charity's independent examiner or auditor.

The Charity Commission expects a cautious approach so, if in doubt, trustees should report any incident that may be considered serious. Guidance on reporting serious incidents is available on the Commission's website.

International transactions

When funds are moved internationally, there are particular risks of loss or misappropriation (e.g. misappropriation for terrorist purposes). Trustees have a responsibility to safeguard charitable funds and assets, and to ensure they are used for legitimate purposes, within the charity's own charitable purposes. Verification of the correct end use of funds transferred overseas is essential. Where possible, it is best to move funds through formal banking systems. If alternative financial systems are to be used, there will be additional matters to consider regarding appropriate financial controls, security, and verification of delivery and end use.

Solvency issues

Ensuring the charity remains solvent is crucial to its financial well-being and to the correct discharge of the trustees' duties. In simple terms, an organisation is solvent if it can pay its debts and liabilities as they fall due (this is the cash flow or 'short-term liquidity' test). An alternative measure of solvency is whether the value of the overall assets exceeds the total liabilities of the organisation (this is the 'balance sheet test'). It is not sufficient for an organisation simply to meet this second test – if it cannot meet the short-term liquidity test, it will face insolvency.

Unincorporated charities, such as unincorporated trusts or unincorporated members' associations, have no separate legal identity of their own, so individual trustees have to make legal commitments for the charity in their own personal capacity (for example, enter into contracts). It is therefore critical that the available assets are always sufficient to cover these personal liabilities.

For the trustees of incorporated charities, the limited liability protection usually prevents them from becoming personally liable for the charity's debts. However, where serious mismanagement precedes insolvent liquidation, the protection can be removed and the trustees held personally liable for 'wrongful trading'. This is rare in practice.

Many organisations that fail financially do so simply because they fail to maintain adequate cash flow. Failure to retain sufficient spendable reserve funds can be a risk to solvency, as can an unexpected major loss of assets, unforeseen major expenditure needs or a sudden significant loss of income.

Charitable funds should never be put at risk in 'propping up' a failing trading subsidiary, nor should restricted funds be misapplied to pay for the charity's general expenditure.

Where trustees are concerned about the charity's ability to continue operating, due to its financial position, they should act immediately. If appropriate corrective action is taken early, it may be possible to rectify the situation. Otherwise, it may be too late to save the charity and the trustees may be at risk of significant personal liabilities. It is important to seek independent professional advice at an early stage rather than trying to manage the situation 'in-house'.

Where closure is under consideration, there will be closure costs to meet, as well as paying creditors. These may include:

- outstanding payments to staff and redundancy costs;
- pension obligations and pension deficits;
- termination fees and other expenses for ending contracts or leases of property; and
- winding-up costs and other necessary legal fees.

Careful records should be made throughout any period of financial instability and during any closure process. This includes details of the trustees' decisions and the reasons for them, as well as details of all professional advice obtained and the trustees' consideration of that advice.

Insurance

Dealing with a charity's insurance is a mix of meeting legal obligations, prudent stewardship of the charity's resources and risk management. Some insurance cover is compulsory, especially in relation to employers' liability and public liability in respect of vehicles.

The law requires employers to have at least £5 million insurance cover in place in relation to diseases that may be contracted, and injuries that may be suffered, by their employees while carrying out their employment duties. This insurance must be obtained from an appropriate regulated insurer and a certificate must be prominently displayed in the workplace, showing that a valid policy is in place, together with the level of cover.

In the case of vehicles, it is compulsory to insure against third-party personal injury or property damage. Special additional requirements apply to certain vehicles, such as minibuses. Where personal vehicles are being used by staff or volunteers on the charity's business, the charity should ensure the owner's insurance covers this use.

When making decisions about what additional, optional insurance cover is appropriate for the charity, careful judgements are needed on various matters:

- Which risks are *this charity's* risks?
- Which of the potentially insurable risks will be retained (effectively self-insured)?
- Which risks can, and will, be transferred by means of insurance? (Note that some risks are best managed by other methods.)
- What is the balance between the likelihood of a major risk becoming reality, the prospective level of harm or loss and the costs of insurance?

Ownership or occupation of land and buildings brings particular risks, especially if there is public access or use. Generally where a charity owns the freehold of a building, it should insure that building for its full reinstatement value. Where the charity leases part of its premises to another organisation, it should try to place obligations on the tenant for insuring the leased area (or funding the cost of the charity insuring that area). Checks should be made to ensure a tenant has made appropriate arrangements if it is the tenant's obligation to insure. Where the charity retains full responsibility, it should ensure the rental level is adequate to recompense the charity for the costs of insuring the leased area.

Where a charity is the lessee of premises, it may be under an obligation to arrange insurance (though that may be limited to particular risks, such as fire). It is important to check and comply with the detailed terms of the lease.

Public liability insurance is particularly important in relation to publicly accessible areas owned by charities or permitted public access to charity premises, and for public events organised by a charity or held on its premises. The occupiers of premises have a legal duty of care to visitors to their property (and even to trespassers).

In order to protect the charity's property, at its own premises, it is clearly prudent to arrange contents insurance. Correct valuation of current replacement costs is important to ensure full recompense for any loss. Charities should consider obtaining an index-linked insurance policy.

There are particular practical and cost challenges in relation to insuring historic buildings and other heritage assets, such as art collections. Some items may be irreplaceable due to their unique nature or the high cost of potential 'replacement value' insurance. Specialist independent advice should be taken to assist the trustees in making reasonable decisions about such matters.

There are a number of specialist charity sector insurance providers who are usually able to provide a suitable package of cost-effective insurance cover to a charity, often in a single policy. Charities should seek at least two alternative quotes. It is also important to check the detail of the cover offered, to ensure it meets the charity's identified needs and avoids duplication (which might invalidate policies).

It is good practice to review the charity's insurance arrangements on an annual basis. Some independent insurance brokers offer free insurance reviews for charities.

Trustees' indemnity insurance

Trustees' indemnity insurance is insurance cover for the trustees, in their personal capacity, against certain personal risks associated with their trusteeship. It is not part of the charity's insurance cover.

Trustees are free to arrange their own personal insurance cover, at their own cost, should they wish to do so. Understandably, this is not common.

A charity may only use charitable funds to pay for trustees' indemnity insurance if its constitution does not specifically forbid this. There are common law and public policy limitations on what liabilities may be insured (e.g. trustees cannot be protected against liability for breaches of trust or criminal liabilities for their own dishonesty). Under Scots charity law, there are various statutory limitations.

Before considering taking out separate trustees' indemnity insurance, it is wise to check what relevant cover may already be included in the charity's own insurance policy – for example, legal expenses cover.

There is little benefit for the trustees of a limited liability charity in having such insurance, since they already have the protections afforded by that limited liability. For trustees of other charities, indemnity insurance cover may reassure them; however, in practice it is rare for any claim to be made and rarer still for one to succeed.

Safeguarding

Safeguarding is about protecting people's health and well-being, especially by ensuring they do not suffer any harm, abuse or neglect. There is a particular need to focus on safeguarding for children, young people and others who are vulnerable because of their needs or circumstances – for instance, age, frailty, disability, substance abuse and addiction problems or homelessness. Good practice in this highly sensitive area should be an absolute priority for charities, focusing on awareness and prevention.

Charities must ensure they comply fully with all applicable legal obligations relevant to, for example, 'regulated activities' where there is close and unsupervised contact between charity staff or volunteers and vulnerable individuals. Trustees must develop and implement appropriate systems and procedures, ensuring these are effective and are being followed in practice by everyone in the charity.

The Disclosure and Barring Service (DBS) is the official government agency that provides criminal records checks to organisations, and fulfils various regulatory and legal functions in relation to people who have been legally barred from carrying out activities, either with children and young people or with other vulnerable people. The Charity Commission's role in safeguarding mainly relates to the conduct of trustees and the adequate discharge of the trustees' overall duty of care in this area. Other official agencies have wider safeguarding responsibilities and deal with incidents and allegations of abuse – for example, the Care Quality Commission (or equivalent agencies in Scotland and Northern Ireland) and the police.

Health and safety

Like any other organisation, a charity has health and safety responsibilities towards its employees, volunteers and others, including contractors that it engages, visitors to its premises, participants in events it organises and the wider public (e.g. in relation to use of the charity's vehicles). Employers have a general responsibility to provide a safe place of work and specific obligations apply in a number of areas, such as fire safety awareness and training.

Reasonable safety precautions should be taken at all times. Above all, these are to protect people from harm but they are also to protect the charity, its trustees and its senior managers from potential legal penalties and liabilities.

Data protection

Gathering, holding and use of information about living individuals is something nearly all charities do, to at least some extent. These activities are subject to data protection law.

There are various legal obligations on those who control data, directing (individually or with others) how and why personal data is processed. These include requirements about protection and security of data, accuracy of the data kept about an individual and proper use of data.

Note that the legal rules apply to electronic data, paper-based data and mixed-media data. Note also that the use of CCTV surveillance and security systems has data protection implications, which can include an obligation to register with the ICO.

There are also particular rules applicable to data processors, who process data on behalf of, and at the direction of, a data controller (and are not employees of the data controller). These rules are aimed at independent contractors engaged to deal with data on behalf of another organisation, so they are relevant where a charity buys data-processing services from a third-party contractor (e.g. processing of a donor database or appeals).

Honest and clear communication is often at the heart of data protection issues, with failures in areas such as:

- obtaining all relevant consents from individuals; and
- providing open communication about what use will be made of data obtained about individuals and why it will be used in that way.

The ICO does sometimes impose substantial financial penalties on charities for data protection compliance failures. It has significant enforcement powers, as well as the power to impose such financial penalties. In addition, a range of criminal sanctions may apply when breaches of data protection law occur.

Charities need to improve their performance in data protection compliance, not only because of the risk of such penalties but also because of the potential reputational damage. The occasional joint alerts issued by the Charity Commission and ICO to charities are useful tools. Charities should also carefully consider the ICO's guidance on particular areas (such as consent) and its charity-specific guidance notes.

Electronic communications and websites

Electronic communications and websites are extremely useful to charities as part of their general communication processes and, increasingly, as one of the ways in which they deliver services to their beneficiaries. Charities should address a variety of legal, administrative and regulatory issues in these areas, including:

- cookies regulations;
- disclosure obligations regarding charity details, which extend to websites and electronic communications by charities (such as texts and e-mails) as well as paper-based material;
- regulations applicable to the use of electronic communications and websites for fundraising and appeals (note this includes phone communications);

- credit card and e-commerce rules, such as the obligation to allow donors to cancel donations made by some methods, within a particular 'cooling-off' period;
- potential inappropriate behaviour by staff or volunteers in their use of electronic media; and
- legal risks such as issues of copyright, trademark infringement or allegations of libel.

There is general legal provision relating to electronic communications and electronic signatures in the Electronic Communications Act 2000.

For companies, there are significant rules in the Companies Act 2006 addressing electronic communications:

- *to* a company *by an individual member* (schedule 4); or
- *by* a company (either to its own members or from a corporate member to the company of which it is a member) (Schedule 5).

The schedules cited above apply regardless of anything in the company's articles. Their requirements are detailed and complex. Care should be taken to interpret and apply them correctly in all formal company/member communications (such as communications relating to general meetings of the members, or communications providing access to the annual accounts and reports of the company).

Note also the Companies Act rules regarding 'authentication' of documents and information – see further comments later in this chapter.

Cookies are small electronic files, commonly used on websites, designed to hold data about a particular user. When a user accesses the website using their device, the cookies are downloaded and stored on that user's electronic device (either temporarily or permanently).

Relevant regulations apply to the use of cookies or websites. These regulations apply to charities. In summary, an organisation must:

- tell people if cookies are being used on its website;
- explain what those cookies are doing; and
- obtain the site user's consent to any cookie that will be stored on their device.

Obtaining consent once is likely to be sufficient, provided the information provided when seeking the consent is clear enough. Burying the consent in a lengthy privacy policy, in the depths of a website, is not an adequate way to deal with the matter.

The Information Commissioner's Office receives significant numbers of public complaints about misuse of cookies and non-compliance with the legal requirements. It regularly checks compliance, especially when members of the public raise concerns. Financial penalties for non-compliance are significant (up to £500,000), with the potential of criminal penalties in addition, so charities should ensure their websites do comply with these requirements.

Execution of documents

How charities execute documents depends on:

- the legal nature of the charity (especially whether or not it is incorporated);
- the terms of the charity's constitution;
- the nature of the transaction to which the document relates (and any special legal rules that may apply to it); and
- the applicable jurisdictional law (whether it is a transaction under the law of England and Wales or Scotland or Northern Ireland).

The above factors affect the level of formality and the detailed procedures required. It is important to observe the correct process, and appropriate legal advice should be taken.

Charitable companies and trading subsidiaries need to observe the terms of their articles when executing any document (e.g. as to authorising the use and countersignature of a company seal). In addition, the Companies Act provisions regarding execution of documents by companies should be noted. Those provisions state that a company can execute a document under the law of England and Wales by:

- fixing the company seal on the document; or
- executing without use of a seal, in accordance with the Companies Act procedures.

Company seal

A company may choose to have a company seal but is not obliged to do so. Initial adoption of a seal should be by formal resolution of the board. Subsequently, the company has a choice of executing documents with its seal or using the Companies Act alternative methods of execution for the particular item.

Use of the seal should be formally authorised, as should the countersignatories; the decisions should be recorded in the minutes of the relevant board meeting. Records should be kept of all items sealed – a register of sealings is useful (though not a statutory requirement). The seal itself should be kept in safe custody.

Execution of documents by companies without a seal under the law of England and Wales

The Companies Act 2006 permits execution of a document by a company under the law of England and Wales, without a seal, if it is signed on behalf of the company by:

- two directors;
- one director and the secretary; or
- one director in the presence of a witness, who attests the director's signature.

The decision to execute is a matter for the whole board, as is the authorisation of the chosen signatories. Note that non-directors (i.e. non-trustees) may not be authorised for this purpose. These decisions should be carefully recorded in the minutes of the relevant board meeting. The company may also choose to keep a non-statutory register of executions.

Execution of deeds: companies

For certain legal transactions and arrangements under the law of England and Wales, it is appropriate or necessary to enter into a deed. A document is validly executed as a deed by a company, for the purposes of section 1(2)(b) of the Law of Property (Miscellaneous Provisions) Act 1989, and for the purposes of the law of Northern Ireland, if it is:

- duly executed; and
- delivered as a deed.

Delivery is presumed on execution unless the contrary is proved. A deed must contain appropriate wording, including in its execution clause.

Execution of documents: other charities

Charities that are incorporated bodies but not companies (e.g. Royal Charter bodies) must follow the procedures required by their own constitutions to execute documents.

A CIO can execute documents under its seal or in accordance with the CIO General Regulations (regulation 20(2)). This alternative method of execution requires the document:

- to be signed by two of the CIOs trustees (or one, if the CIO only has one trustee); and
- to be expressed as being executed by the CIO.

Unincorporated charities execute documents (including deeds) in accordance with their own constitutions (usually by signature of all the trustees).

There is also a statutory power for the trustees of an unincorporated charity to authorise any two or more of the trustees to execute documents in the names of, and on behalf of, the trustees to give effect to a transaction to which all the trustees are a party (section 333 of the Charities Act 2011). The authority conferred may be general or limited as specified in the relevant trustees' decision (e.g. authority to execute a specific document, rather than documents in general). A further advantage of this procedure is that it avoids having to join in new trustees to a deed previously signed by all the former trustees.

Execution of documents under the law of Scotland

The law of Scotland makes different provision for the execution of documents. The key provisions are in the Requirements of Writing (Scotland) Act 1995 and, in the context of companies, section 48 of the Companies Act 2006. Specific Scots legal advice should be taken where appropriate.

Records of sealings and executions

Board decisions to enter into contracts, authorise the use of the charity's seal or otherwise authorise execution of documents (including deeds) should be properly recorded in the minutes of the relevant board meeting. Where specific signatories are authorised, the minutes should include details of that decision and the names of the relevant individuals.

It is good practice to record each use of the seal, or execution of a document without a seal, in an optional register of sealings and executions, and to ensure a full copy of the sealed or executed document is also retained.

Authentication of documents and information: Companies Act 2006 rules

The Companies Act 2006 uses the term 'authenticated' widely in relation to documents and information sent to a person by a company or supplied by a person to a company. It does so for both hard copy and electronic formats. The legal rules specify:

- a hard copy item is authenticated if it is signed by the person sending or supplying it.
- an item in electronic form is authenticated if:
  - the identity of the sender is confirmed in a manner prescribed by the company; or
  - where no such manner has been specified, if the communication contains or is accompanied by a statement of the identity of the sender and the company has no reason to doubt the truth of that statement.

(See section 1146 of the Companies Act 2006.)

Registers and records

While unincorporated members' associations will normally keep some form of membership records (and are strongly advised to do so, for obvious reasons), there are no statutory requirements about the form and content of those records. The individual organisation's constitution may include some specific requirements and if it does, those should be followed.

Some other legal forms of charity are required to keep registers under specific statutory requirements (especially charitable companies, CIOs and SCIOs).

Other records may be necessary because of general legal provisions, such as health and safety or employment legislation.

Statutory registers: companies

A private company must keep statutory registers that comply with company law requirements. These legal requirements apply equally to charitable companies and the trading subsidiaries of charities.

Registers can be kept in paper form in bound books or loose-leaf formats. Computer systems may also be used provided the registers can be reproduced in legible form. Whatever methods are chosen, the company must take adequate security steps to prevent and detect falsification or accidental loss or damage.

Register of members: companies

For each member, the details required are: name, address and dates of admission/cessation of membership. With the exception of the initial subscribers on incorporation, the only persons who are members of the company are those who have agreed to be members and whose names have been entered in the register of members. Accordingly this register can be vital if doubts arise over who the members are.

It is essential that the register of members is accurate and up to date. The register will need to be consulted for the proper corporate administration of the charity – for example, when formally contacting members or verifying who is entitled to attend and vote at any annual or other general meeting.

A company must be careful to record in its register of members all those who are its members for the purposes of company law. However, other persons associated with the company but who are not members in law (e.g. 'supporters' or 'associates', or directors/trustees who are not legal members) should not be recorded in this register. Separate records should be kept for such groups of people.

Registers of directors and secretary: companies

For directors, their name, an address, date of birth and business occupation (if any) must be specified, plus dates of appointment to and cessation of office. The address can be either their home address or a 'service address'. The service address can be simply stated as 'the registered office'.

Details of 'other directorships' are not required, but the director does have to give any name(s) by which they are or were known for business purposes. There is no longer an exception for a married woman's former name. The Companies Act 2006 requires a director's usual country or state of residence, or the part of the UK in which they are usually resident, to be recorded.

For any secretary, their name, an address, and dates of appointment and cessation of office must be recorded. Again, the address can be either their home address or a 'service address'.

Register of Directors' Residential Addresses (RODRA): companies

To support the rights of privacy for individual directors' residential addresses, companies must keep records of individual directors' residential addresses in the RODRA. This is not open to general public access (though various investigatory and regulatory bodies have access rights).

If the director has already entered their residential address as their service address in the Register of Directors, the RODRA need only state that fact. The exception is if the director's residential address is the registered office address, and the address given as the service address is 'the company's registered office'. In that case, the address must be given in full in the RODRA.

Register of charges: companies

This must contain details of all charges that are subject to registration requirements.

Register of persons with significant control: companies

Amendments to the Companies Act made by the Small Business, Enterprise and Employment Act 2015 require companies to keep a register of persons with significant control (PSCs).

An individual is a PSC if:

- directly or indirectly they own or control 25% of the voting rights of member (or 25% of the shares, in a company limited by shares);
- directly or indirectly they have control over the appointment and removal of a majority of the board of directors; or
- they otherwise have significant influence over the company.

The register must contain these details about a PSC:

- name
- date of birth
- nationality
- country, state or part of the UK where that person usually lives
- service address
- usual residential address*
- the date that person became a PSC in relation to the company (or 6 April 2016 for companies that already had PSCs when the obligation to keep this register came into effect) and
- which conditions for being a PSC are met by that person.

*This information is not available to the public and should not be revealed to anyone in response to a public inspection request. A number of investigatory and other official agencies and bodies have the legal right to access the address information.

Subject to the protection of the residential address details above, the register is open to public access. If an access request is made by anyone, the company must make the register available at the company's registered office (or provide copies if requested to do so).

Service addresses for members, directors and secretary: companies

A service address for an individual director can be recorded in the public part of the register of directors, with the residential address kept separately in the 'register of directors' residential addresses'. A range of regulatory and investigatory agencies can access that, but it is not open to general public inspection.

Where the residential address is not also the service address then the residential address or, where the service address is also the residential address, the fact that it is, is called 'protected information' in the Companies Act 2006. These details remain protected information even after a director has ceased to hold office, so that references to a director include a former director.

Note that the residential address still has to be supplied to the Registrar of Companies. It is kept securely, with access available only to relevant authorities and credit reference agencies. The Registrar of Companies is, however, only required to protect residential addresses given officially and correctly. They are under no obligation to check that a residential address has not been given inadvertently – for example, in the presenter's details on a statutory form.

A third party may want to know a director's residential address (either that a separate residential address has been given, or that the service address given is also the director's residential address). The circumstances in which this protected information may be disclosed (or used) by Companies House are:

- a residential address may be used to communicate with the director;
- the protected information may be disclosed to a public authority specified in regulations;

- the protected information may be disclosed to a credit reference agency (as defined in the Consumer Credit Act 1974); or
- if a director consents to disclosure.

The secretary of state has made regulations setting out conditions that must be satisfied before such a disclosure may be made (Companies (Disclosure of Address) Regulations 2009). These include reassurances about the security measures the agency has in place to protect the data and declarations about the purposes for which it is being sought.

The regulations also set out the circumstances in which application can be made to prevent disclosure to a credit reference agency. Essentially there has to be risk of serious violence against the director or someone in their household in order to gain this added protection.

If a service address is ineffective, the Registrar of Companies can put the residential address on the public record, provided that they have sent a warning notice to the director and every company of which the individual is director. The notice must be sent to the residential address unless it appears to the Registrar that service there may be ineffective to bring it to the director's attention, in which case the Registrar can use the service address. The notice must specify the grounds upon which the Registrar proposes to put the residential address on the public record, and the period during which the director may make representations as to why their residential address should not be disclosed. If they make representations, the Registrar must consider these.

If the Registrar decides to put the residential address on the public record, Companies House updates the public record as if it has been notified that the service address is the director's home address. Companies House must then notify the director, and the company. The company must amend its statutory registers to include the director's residential address. If the director has notified the company of a more recent residential address, that address must be entered in its registers, and a change of particulars filed with the Registrar. The director is then prohibited from using a service address that is not their residential address for the next five years.

Location and inspection of statutory registers: companies

The default position is that a company must keep its registers available for inspection at its registered office. However, regulations made under the Companies Act 2006 allow a company to specify a single alternative inspection location (SAIL), as an alternative to the registered office, where it may keep all or any of its public records available for inspection.

The conditions that must be met in order to use a SAIL are as follows:

1 The SAIL is situated in the part of the UK in which the company is registered.
2 The company notifies Companies House of that SAIL (form AD02).
3 The company notifies Companies House which records are kept at the SAIL (form AD03).

All records of a given type must be kept together, either at a SAIL or the registered office; they cannot be split between two locations.

A company must, within five working days, disclose the address of its registered office, and any address where it keeps company records available for public inspection (and the type of company records kept there), to any person it deals with in the course of its business who makes a written request to the company for that information. It must also state the SAIL address (if any), and which records are kept at the SAIL as at the return date.

The regulations require a person wishing to inspect the company's records to give the company advance notice. The notice period is generally ten days, but is two days in certain specified circumstances. The records must be available for inspection on any working day for at least two hours between 9.00am and 3.00pm.

The current rules on access to and inspection of the register of members retain the general principle of public access to the register of members but also provide safeguards against potential abuses of the access right. The following rules apply to any request for access:

- The request must provide the name and address of the person making it.
- The request must say what the information will be used for, whether it will be shared with anyone else and, if so, whom and for what purpose.

The company has five days to comply with the request (or to seek a court order that the request is not made for a proper purpose). The Companies Act 2006 leaves decisions about what would, or would not, be a proper purpose to the courts, where any application is made to refuse an access request.

Helpful guidance has been issued by ICSA analysing matters that may reasonably be considered to be proper or improper purposes in the context of register of members' access requests (Guidance Note: Access to the Register of Members).

A Court of Appeal decision (Burry & Knight Limited & Another v Knight 2014) has indicated that:

- where a request is made for multiple purposes, some of which are proper and some not, the company does not have to provide access;
- where a company member (rather than a member of the public) requests access, a proper purpose ought generally to relate to that person's interest in their capacity as a member;
- if a member requests access in order to communicate with other members, a strong case would be needed for the court to exercise its discretion to prevent access; and
- while the ICSA guidance is neither binding nor exhaustive, courts might have regard to it when considering applications to refuse access requests.

Registers: CIOs and SCIOs

CIOs and SCIOs must keep a register of trustees and a register of members.

Relevant regulations require particular information to be recorded in these registers; however, there is no set format, so a CIO or SCIO may keep the required details in whatever format it finds convenient. Appropriate arrangements should be made to safeguard the registers against loss, accidental damage, falsification and theft.

There is general public access to the register of trustees. Restrictions apply to the register of members which can only be accessed by the members themselves, the trustees, and various public, regulatory and investigatory bodies.

Records of meetings

Charities should always keep records of formal meetings, both trustees' meetings and meetings of their members, such as the annual general meeting. These are usually kept as minutes. Any company is obliged to keep such records by Companies Act requirements. These records must be kept for a minimum of ten years (indefinitely for minutes of meetings held before 1 October 2008).

Records of general meetings of the members of a company must be kept at the registered office and can be inspected by any member as well as any director and the company's auditor (if it has an auditor).

Board meeting records can be kept wherever the board deems appropriate, but are only available for inspection by members of the board and the auditors. Members have no statutory right of access.

Minutes of meetings should be accurate, brief and complete. They should also be principally minutes of record – a formal legal record of decisions taken by the relevant meeting. Sometimes minutes of narration will be appropriate – for example, the principal elements of a discussion that preceded a complex, difficult or particularly important decision, or the board's reasons for determining a particular course of action (such as financial evidence of the need for, or consequences of, that action). Any document cross-referred to in the minutes should always be retained with them in original or copy form as appropriate (e.g. a budget/cash flow forecast/or a copy of a document authorised to be sealed or executed).

If a company's minutes of board or members' meetings are 'authenticated' by the chairman of the meeting in question (or the chairman of the next meeting), they are *prima facie* evidence of the matters they record. The Companies Act 2006 permits electronic authentication methods and also allows traditional signature of a hard copy.

All charities should ensure that the authorisation procedures, access facilities (including remote electronic access) and the storage arrangements they choose in relation to minutes are appropriate and adequate (in relation to accidental loss and damage, falsification, unauthorised access, etc).

Disclosure obligations

Disclosure obligations exist for charities as part of the 'quid pro quo' for the benefits they enjoy through their special legal status (such as charity tax exemptions and the protection of limited liability for the members of charitable companies, CIOs and SCIOs). There is a valid public interest to be served by ensuring third parties are aware they are dealing with a charity, and by ensuring they can identify that entity correctly and establish certain key legal information about it. This is also part of the overall public accountability regime for charities.

Charity disclosure obligations: England and Wales

All charities registered in England and Wales with incomes exceeding £10,000 have to state that they are a registered charity on:

- notices, advertisements or other documents issued by or on behalf of the charity that solicit money or property for the charity's benefit;
- bills of exchange, promissory notes, endorsements, cheques and orders for money or goods purporting to be signed on the charity's behalf; and
- bills, invoices, receipts and letters of credit.

Best practice is to state 'registered charity in England and Wales number XXXXXX'. The statement must be in English (except for Welsh charities, which can use Welsh); however, if the charity normally uses another language, the statement can appear in both English and that other language. The printing must be in legible characters.

Anyone who signs or issues or authorises the issue of a non-compliant item is liable to criminal penalties (fines) whether or not they did so knowingly – it is a strict liability offence.

Charity disclosure obligations: Scotland

For charities subject to regulation in Scotland, regulations require a range of disclosures to be made (see the Charities References in Documents (Scotland) Regulations 2007 as amended). In summary, these require inclusion on a wide range of documents of:

- the Scottish charity registration number;
- the name by which the charity is recorded on the Scottish Charity Register; and
- an indication of the charity's charitable status (if the word 'charity' or 'charitable' is not part of its name).

Relevant documents include letters, e-mails, adverts, notices and official publications, items soliciting money or property, invoices, receipts, accounts, campaign and educational documentation, and documents relating to land transactions and contracts.

The OSCR has issued helpful guidance on the application of the Scots law rules; this can be viewed at www.oscr.org.uk.

Note that an English charity also registered in Scotland must comply with both the English and the Scottish disclosure requirements.

Company disclosure obligations

Company law applies disclosure obligations to all companies. For charitable companies, these obligations are in addition to their charity law disclosure obligations.

For the purposes of Tables 5 and 6 below, 'company name' means the name of the company as on the company's certificate of incorporation, including 'Limited' or 'Ltd' (or their Welsh equivalents) and 'where registered' means 'England and Wales', 'Scotland' or 'Northern Ireland' according to the location of the registered office.

Whether on stationery, websites or premises, all disclosures must be in characters that can be read with the naked eye.

Table 4: Stationery, websites, etc.

	Company name	Where registered	Registered office address	Company number
Business letters	✓	✓	✓	✓
Order forms	✓	✓	✓	✓
Orders for goods, services or money	✓	✓	✓	✓
Cheques	✓			
Invoices and receipts	✓			
Notices and official publications	✓			
Bills of exchange, promissory notes, endorsements, bills of parcel and letters of credit	✓			
Written demands for payment of debts	✓			
Websites, order forms, e-mails and other electronic documents	✓	✓	✓	✓
Applications for licences to carry on a trade or activity	✓			

At premises, details must be positioned so they can be seen easily by visitors.

There is no legal requirement for the company to display its certificate of incorporation at its registered office or any other premises.

Table 5: Premises

	Company name
The company's registered office (unless the company has always been dormant)	✓
Any 'inspection place', i.e. any location (other than the registered office) where the company keeps any company record available for public inspection (unless the company has always been dormant)	✓
Every location in which the company carries on business that is not the registered office or an 'inspection place' (unless primarily used for living accommodation, or unless every director is protected from disclosure of their residential address to a credit reference agency)	✓

Statement of limited liability status

A charitable company that has been granted permission to omit 'limited' from its name under the Companies Act 2006 (or the previous Companies Act 1985 rules) must state that it is a limited company on all business letters and order forms. The statement must be in English and in legible characters; the usual form is 'A company limited by guarantee'.

Additional disclosure obligations: CIOs and SCIOs

CIOs and SCIOs are subject to some additional disclosure obligations under relevant regulations, including a requirement to state their CIO or SCIO status in certain documents and communications.

CIOs and SCIOs cannot omit 'CIO' (or Charitable Incorporated Organisation) or 'SCIO' (or Scottish Charitable Incorporated Organisation) from the end of their names.

Other disclosures

Other legislation may impose additional requirements on charities; these may be particularly relevant to stationery items. For example, if the organisation is registered for VAT, the VAT registration number must be shown on invoices and receipts.

Disclosures: practicalities and issues

Deciding which items are subject to a given set of legal rules is not always easy. Paper letter heading, invoices, receipts, demands for payment, orders for goods and services are certainly stationery items subject to relevant rules. However, e-mails, faxes, other forms of electronic communication, websites, compliments slips and business cards can be more problematic – at times it may depend on how they are used. For instance, such items could be used either to place or receive an order or to record a contract between a third party and the organisation. A cautious approach is to include full statutory details on these 'problem' items.

Guidance should be given to staff, volunteers and local branches or remote offices that may be ordering or using stationery items (e.g. local event posters, fundraising literature, local group letter heading) or sending electronic communications on behalf of the charity.

Independent groups or bodies should not be allowed to use a charity's name and charity registration number in a manner that might mislead the public into believing they are dealing with the charity itself, rather than a separate organisation.

If there are any changes of name, care should be taken to ensure all old stationery is withdrawn and new stationery is used from the date of the change. Other items will also require attention, including electronic communications and websites. There are risks if this is not adequately dealt with – for instance, potential criminal penalties or personal liabilities for directors or trustees or any secretary of a charitable company, CIO or SCIO if a cheque or certain other documents are issued in the incorrect name.

Correct timing of such changes is important. A charitable company's name only changes in law when the certificate of incorporation on change of name is issued (not on the date the change of name resolution is passed). Changes of name in unincorporated charities usually take immediate effect as the relevant change of name resolution is passed.

Legal administration

The precise requirements for the legal administration of a charity will depend on its legal form, specific legislative requirements for that legal form, any additional special legal status it has (e.g. as a registered care home or a registered social landlord) and the specific legislative requirements that flow from that status. It will also in part be affected by the provisions of the individual organisation's constitution.

All charities must also comply with the legal administrative requirements of the general law in areas such as employment, insurance, tax and VAT, health and safety, data protection and much else. This has particular importance in the context of recordkeeping and the practical operation of the organisation.

8 Resourcing the charity: funding and fundraising

Funding

Most charities rely on funding from a mix of sources, including voluntary income and a significant proportion of self-generated income. Voluntary income usually includes one-off donations from members of the public and some regular committed giving from supporters of the charity – for example, by monthly direct debit.

Legacies are also an important source of voluntary income for some charities. Some health-related charities receive as much as 40–60% of their annual income from legacies. However, there is considerable scope for improvement, as many charities still receive few, or no, legacies and only about one-third of the UK population actually make a will. Of those who do, only about 4% include a legacy to one or more charities in their will.

A gift in a will to a charity may be a specific item, such as shares, or a fixed sum (known as a 'pecuniary legacy'). Alternatively, after payment of taxes and the costs of administration and payment of any specific legacies to the relevant beneficiaries, the will may have the net balance of the estate as a 'residuary legacy' to one or more charities. An individual's will should be reviewed periodically and whenever a major event occurs, such as a marriage or the birth of a child.

Self-generated income may be directly earned income, arising from charges made by the charity in relation to its direct charitable activities (e.g. a charitable art gallery selling tickets to an exhibition or a charitable theatre selling tickets to a performance). Around 46% of all registered charity sector income in England and Wales is now income generated by direct charitable activities. Alternatively, self-generated income may arise from fundraising trading, either trading undertaken directly by the charity, within the relevant tax thresholds, or generated by the trading activities of the charity's trading subsidiary and passed up to the parent charity by a Gift Aid donation.

Charities may also operate specific fundraising activities to generate income (draws or lotteries, fundraising events, etc). Membership charities will usually obtain some income by charging annual membership fees to their members.

Loan funding is a potential source of temporary income, perhaps arranged as part of the funding package to acquire or refurbish a building. It is important to recognise that loans must be repaid in accordance with the agreed terms (they are not gifts) so a charity that has taken out a loan has to manage its finances sufficiently well to generate enough income to meet those repayments. There are various legal restrictions and obligations relevant to charity borrowings and the granting of security by a charity (dealt with later in this chapter).

Some grant funding remains available, though this is now mainly limited to grants from other charities such as charitable grant-making trusts.

While it was once common for charities to receive significant sums of direct public funding through grants, especially charities operating in areas such as healthcare, social welfare and social housing, this is no longer the case. The reductions in public spending, both centrally and at local government level, combined with prolonged and severe economic difficulties in the UK and beyond, have led to drastic reductions in public spending and driven forward major reforms in the delivery of public services and the custody and care of public assets. Consequently, it is now far more common for charities to be involved with provision of contracted public services (in return for fees) or custodianship of community assets, formerly held in public ownership.

Tax-efficient giving

The range of tax exemptions and reliefs available on certain gifts to charities are valuable and can enhance the charity's income. A charity should seek to use them as widely as possible, to:

- encourage giving, by reducing the cost to the donor of making the gift (tax relief is not a *major* motivator for donors but is a consideration for at least some); and
- maximise the value of gifts to the charity from both individuals and businesses.

When considering tax-efficient giving to charities, donors should seek independent tax and legal advice, since personal circumstances vary.

HMRC guidance

HMRC provides very helpful general information about tax-efficient giving to charities on its website, both for individuals considering how best to help their chosen charities and for the charities themselves, seeking to encourage donors to give in the most effective ways and to make the most of the charity tax reliefs and exemptions available to them. The guidance includes information about Gift Aid and model Gift Aid declarations and giving to charities by will.

Tax-efficient giving: individuals

There are potential tax reliefs for the donor on gifts of land, certain other property and qualifying shares to charities. Some of these apply to gifts made during the donor's lifetime, while others are available on death and apply to the donor's estate in relation to charitable gifts made in the deceased's will.

There are strict limits on the level of any benefits that a donor can potentially receive when making tax-efficient gifts to charities. There are also various anti-avoidance measures, intended to prevent abuse of tax relief for charitable giving.

Payroll Giving scheme

Individuals who pay income tax under the PAYE scheme may be able to make tax-efficient gifts to charities by payroll deductions, if their employer has opted to join the Payroll Giving scheme. Guidance on the Payroll Giving scheme and a list of some approved agents who help employers operate such schemes and promote them to their employees can be found on the government's website.

Gift Aid scheme

Donations made by taxpaying individuals under the Gift Aid scheme enable the recipient charity to reclaim the basic rate of tax paid by the donor on the sum given out of their taxed income. A higher-rate taxpayer can also claim a certain amount of tax relief on part of their additional tax liability.

A range of conditions apply where donations are made by individuals under the Gift Aid scheme, including the following:

- There must be an outright gift (e.g. ticket sales to a charity fundraising event will not qualify).

- The gift must be a cash gift (not a gift of assets).
- The donor must be a UK taxpayer, who will pay sufficient direct tax during the relevant tax year to cover all their Gift Aid donations to charities (payments of council tax and indirect taxes, such as VAT, are excluded from this calculation).
- The donor must provide a Gift Aid declaration including all the required information (a model is available on HMRC's website).
- The charity must keep required records of both the donation and any tax reclaim made in respect of it.

In order to benefit from Gift Aid donations, a charity must be registered for the Gift Aid scheme. Guidance is available on HMRC's website: www.gov.uk/charities-and-tax.

Gifts under a will

Generally, a gift to a charity in a will is free of tax and the value of the gift is deducted from the estate for the purposes of calculating the amount of inheritance tax payable on the rest of that estate. Under a special additional tax relief, intended to encourage legacy giving to charities, if a death occurs on or after 6 April 2012 and the deceased's will left at least 10% of their estate to one or more charities, the overall inheritance tax rate applicable to the net estate can be reduced to 36% instead of 40%.

Tax-efficient giving: companies

Companies can make donations to charities under the Gift Aid scheme, provided the gift meets relevant conditions. This benefits both the donor and the charity as the gift is made from pre-tax profits, so the amount given is deducted from the overall profits when calculating the company's corporation tax liability and the charity receives the full gross sum (without having to make a tax reclaim). The conditions include:

- a requirement that the payment is a genuine gift (it cannot be repayable);
- that the relief is claimed during the accounting period in which the gift is made (unless the donor company is a subsidiary owned by one or more charities, in which case a nine-month time limit applies); and
- any benefits to the donor or any 'connected' persons are within specified limits.

Tax-efficient giving: Scotland

The Scotland Act 2012 enables a Scottish rate of income tax to be set by the Scottish Government, and makes other tax changes relevant to Scotland. This has a number of consequences for tax relief on giving to charities by individuals who are taxpayers in Scotland.

The UK Government has recognised the likely administrative burden on charities regarding Gift Aid administration and reclaims, if charities were obliged to operate separate systems for their Scottish donors due to the variation in income tax rates. It has announced that Gift Aid repayments for charities will continue to apply at the UK basic rate, regardless of the tax position of the donor. This will be reviewed if the rates diverge considerably in the future, or if it becomes possible to provide Gift Aid relief for charities at the Scotland-specific rate, alongside the different general UK rate, without placing undue and disproportionate burdens on charities.

Tax relief for Scottish taxpayer donors on their gifts to charities (under the Gift Aid scheme or otherwise) will now be calculated by reference to Scottish tax rates.

Fundraising

Some charities, in particular some grant-making charitable trusts with significant investment income, do not need to actively fundraise. However, this is an increasingly rare situation, so most charities undertake some form of fundraising activity to generate income for their charitable activities and to fund their running costs. For many charities, fundraising is their main, or only, source of income.

Trustees' duties and responsibilities

In relation to fundraising, trustees must understand their role in the context of their general legal duties as charity trustees (see Chapter Three). Ensuring the charity has sufficient resources to carry out its activities and maintaining solvency are key responsibilities of charity trustees, so fundraising is clearly an area that requires the board's attention. Protecting the charity's reputation and ensuring compliance with all relevant legal and regulatory requirements are also crucial aspects of the board's role, in the context of fundraising.

Charity Commission's role

The Commission has significant expectations that trustees will ensure safe, honest and lawful fundraising is carried out, at all times, by their charities. It also expects trustees to consider and take careful note of the Commission's guidance on fundraising, when planning their charity's overall approach to fundraising and ensuring all fundraising undertaken on behalf of the charity is carried out within those parameters.

The Charity Commission has a protective role in the context of funds raised for charitable purposes, which is focused on ensuring the safe custody and correct application of those funds for the charitable purposes for which they were given. Where necessary, the Commission can use some of its intervention powers for the protection of charitable funds. In practice, this would only occur if the risk was serious, the circumstances fell directly in the Commission's particular regulatory remit and no other official agency, investigatory or regulatory body had a more direct role.

Charity Commission guidance

The Charity Commission's guidance on fundraising: Charity Fundraising: A Guide to Trustee Duties [CC20] emphasises that trustees always have overall legal responsibility for all fundraising done by their charity, whether or not they are actively involved in carrying out the fundraising activities themselves.

The guidance specifies that:

'Operating effective control over your charity's fundraising is a vital part of your compliance with your legal duties.'

It sets out six core principles for trustees in relation to fundraising:

1 Effective planning – the trustees must agree and monitor the charity's overall approach to fundraising. In doing so the regulator expects trustees to take into account the charity's values and its relationships with its donors and the wider public, as well as risks and income needs and expectations.

2 Supervision of fundraisers – to ensure their activities are being conducted in a way that furthers the charity's best interests. The regulator expects this oversight for staff and volunteers within the charity and also for third-party agents and contractors involved in fundraising activities for the charity.

3 Protection of the charity's reputation, funds and other assets – here

strong overall management is expected to ensure all funds due to the charity do reach it and that reputational as well as other risks are properly managed. The regulator also expects the trustees to ensure anti-fraud measures are adequate and effective.

4 Ensuring compliance with laws and regulations applicable to the kinds of fundraising being undertaken.

5 Identification and adherence to any codes of practice relevant to the fundraising being carried out (especially the relevant parts of the Code of Fundraising Practice).

6 Commitment to openness and accountability – the regulator has an expectation that trustees will lead in creating a culture of transparency in their charity (this should result in actions well beyond mere compliance with the technical rules on public reporting of fundraising).

The Charity Commission expects trustees to take an active leadership role in relation to fundraising and retain effective adequate oversight of all fundraising, including appeals. It also points out that the trustees must ensure all fundraising appeals are in the best interests of the charity and should actively monitor the performance of appeals against relevant targets.

The regulator also expects the trustees to ensure there is proper control over the fundraising activities and the funds raised, urging particular care if third parties are carrying out the fundraising (paid or unpaid).

In addition, relevant Charity Commission guidance stresses the importance of ensuring the funds are spent on the purposes for which they were raised. That is particularly important when the nature of the appeal for funds means that the funds raised are restricted purpose funds.

The Commission strongly encourages charities that undertake fundraising to follow relevant codes of good practice and to have an open and accessible complaints process available to deal with any complaints that may arise.

The Commission's fundraising guidance emphasises that the charity is answerable for its fundraising and should have:

> ... effective systems in place so that [its] fundraising is explained clearly and openly, fully complies with accounting and reporting obligations, and is appropriately open to challenge by complainants. [CC20]

It also reminds trustees that:

> Every registered charity must produce an annual report and accounts that explain where its money comes from and how the charity expended the funds.

Code of Fundraising Practice

The Code of Fundraising Practice sets out recognised standards for charity fundraising. The Code is overseen by the Fundraising Regulator to maintain independence from the fundraising sector and those engaged in that sector.

The Charity Commission expects charities to comply with the Code standards when carrying out fundraising directly or when authorising and permitting others to do so on their behalf.

Under the Code, all fundraising should adhere to the four overarching principles of being:

1 legal
2 open
3 honest
4 respectful.

The Code is supported by two rulebooks for fundraisers engaging in particular areas of fundraising activity:

1 The Street Fundraising Rulebook sets out the standards of conduct expected of fundraisers who engage with the public in publicly accessible local areas (including on the street). These require fundraisers to respect the public and the fundraising environment, to safeguard the public (especially those who are vulnerable) and inform the public clearly about matters such as who the fundraiser works for, how that organisation will be paid, what length of commitment is being sought from the donor and what the financial nature of the 'ask' is.

2. The Door to Door Fundraising Rulebook deals with matters such as approaching households respectfully, the times of day during which fundraisers may knock on doors/ring doorbells etc and responsibilities regarding observing 'no-calling zones' and no-calling door stickers.

Fundraising costs

There is no set minimum amount that a charity should spend on fundraising and likewise no formal maximum amount or percentage that is acceptable for the costs of fundraising. In its fundraising guidance, the Charity Commission recognises that different types of fundraising will involve different sorts of costs and varying levels of costs. The key issue is that the charity's trustees both manage and explain fundraising costs properly.

In doing so, the regulator expects the trustees to:

- be satisfied that the costs are in the charity's best interests;
- be transparent about what fundraising costs were incurred;
- explain those costs clearly (what they are and why they were incurred);
- explain how the funds raised were then spent; and
- articulate why all of this is in the charity's best interests – the charity needs to communicate clearly how it works and why its fundraising costs are necessary.

The Charity Commission expects trustees to distinguish general administrative costs from fundraising costs. It also expects them to have proper systems in place for setting and monitoring fundraising costs. In deciding whether potential cost levels are justifiable, the regulator expects the trustees to weigh the amounts expected to be raised and other benefits to the charity against the projected cost levels, to ensure that balance is proportionate.

Particular fundraising activities – law and regulation

These particular charity fundraising activities are subject to specific charity law and regulation:

- Public collections
- Door-to-door collections
- Event fundraising
- Online, broadcast and telephone fundraising
- Fundraising involving:
  - children
  - fundraisers paid by the charity (who are not professional fundraisers)

- gaming activities (e.g. lotteries, raffles, etc) and
- 'professional fundraisers' or 'commercial participators'.

Many other legal rules can impact on fundraising ventures and initiatives. Obvious examples include law and regulations relating to broadcasting, telecommunications and e-commerce, data protection, the protection of children and vulnerable people, consumer protection laws (particularly important for sales catalogues, shops etc), travel bonding, tour operator and package holiday regulations, insurance and health and safety requirements (particularly important when an overseas 'challenge' event is being considered).

Tax and VAT

Most forms of donations to charities are not subject to tax or VAT. However, care should be taken as there may be tax or VAT considerations in relation to some fundraising – for example, major fundraising events, for which tickets are sold and major corporate 'sponsorship' is obtained, or certain other promotional arrangements with major corporate supporters.

Public fundraising

The charity sector's fundraising self-regulatory regime is of increasing importance to public fundraising, especially in the contexts of fundraising from individuals, protection of vulnerable donors and potential donors, all kinds of fundraising appeals to the public and all types of fundraising in public places or at locations or events to which the public have access. Adherence to the good practice standards set out in the Code of Fundraising Practice is also of increasing importance in all kinds of public fundraising.

The Charity Commission recognises the importance of fundraising as a source of income for charities. It also points out that the public expect charities to raise money in a considerate and responsible way and then to use the funds raised effectively. The regulator's fundraising guidance (see above) reminds charities that the public's trust and generosity should not be taken for granted.

The Commission intends its guidance to help charities fundraise effectively, efficiently and legally, complying with the law and good practice in their fundraising. It encourages charity trustees, staff and all relevant volunteers to use its guidance and also suggests that professional fundraisers, businesses and consultants involved in fundraising and charity donors should also do so.

The Charity Commission also recognises that concerns relating to fundraising practices, relationships with potential and actual donors and the proper use of funds raised by charities are critical drivers of public confidence and trust. The regulator acknowledges that it is discharging its own regulatory role in a context where public expectation of charities:

- demands greater accountability;
- gives less 'benefit of the doubt' to charities and their trustees; and
- increasingly emphasises higher moral and ethical standards, beyond mere legal compliance.

The independent research into public confidence and trust that the Commission arranges, as well as the Commission's own compliance casework, evidence this significant change of climate in public expectations and perceptions. The regulator also recognises that intense media scrutiny and criticism of the charity sector, especially (though not exclusively) in matters relating to public fundraising, charities' relationships with commercial organisations and debates over charity staff remuneration and benefits, add to the growing public demands in the three areas listed above.

All of this has contributed to a firm expectation on the part of the Charity Commission that charity trustees will set parameters for their charity's strategy and practices in fundraising and will actively ensure those parameters are adhered to by all involved in fundraising for the charity. Adequate oversight as well as appropriate challenge by the trustee board is considered essential.

There is also an equally firm expectation that charities will adhere to good practice in fundraising, particular when fundraising from the public and when engaging in fundraising ventures with third parties, including commercial organisations and fundraising businesses.

Public fundraising – communications

Charities should think carefully about how they present appeals for funds to the public, in order to avoid misleading potential donors or setting unrealistic expectations about how the funds will be used and what can be achieved – for instance, with a particular level of donation. Where an appeal seeks funds for a specific purpose (e.g. building an extension to a hospice) gifts made to that appeal are restricted funds and may only be spent on that stated purpose.

Charities should be honest with their donors and with the public in general, about their fundraising activities and the associated costs. Misleading statements suggesting fundraising is entirely cost free, such as 'Every £1 you give goes direct to [helping sick children]' or 'our fundraising does not cost us anything', should be avoided. Instead, clear and accurate information should be given to current and potential supporters, encouraging them to recognise that there are inevitable costs involved in fundraising activities.

Compliance with both data protection law and data protection principles is essential in the context of all fundraising communications activity.

Regulation of fundraising

Modern regulatory regimes are being introduced to regulate public fundraising for charities in all the UK jurisdictions. However, progress has been slow, with Scotland the furthest advanced.

Public collections on behalf of charities: England and Wales

In England and Wales, public collections such as door-to-door and street collections of cash are largely subject to a local authority-based licensing regime. There are special provisions for nationwide collections by major charities, such as the Poppy Appeal for the Royal British Legion.

Fundraising regulations: England and Wales

The main current fundraising regulations relevant to England and Wales flow largely from Part II of the Charities Act 1992 and associated regulations. Some changes have been made by more recent statutory provisions – in particular the requirements for statements to potential donors to be made by professional fundraisers and commercial participators fundraising for charities – enhancing and clarifying the regulations.

These current regulations address fundraising by professional fundraisers and commercial participators.

A professional fundraiser is a person who carries on a fundraising business. That is a business carried on for gain that is wholly or primarily engaged in soliciting or otherwise procuring money or other property for charitable, benevolent or philanthropic purposes. In addition, any other person who, for reward, solicits money or other property for the benefit of a charitable institution is a professional fundraiser.

There are exceptions from the definition of professional fundraiser for:

- charitable institutions themselves;
- companies connected with charitable institutions (so most trading subsidiaries of charities are exempt, provided the charity, alone or with other charities, controls the voting rights at general meetings);
- officers, employees and trustees of charities, acting in those capacities;
- collectors in public charitable collections;
- people paid very small levels of remuneration (under £10 a day and £1,000 a year); and
- people making broadcast appeals for charities (e.g. during TV or radio programmes).

A commercial participator is someone who carries on a non-fundraising business and, in the course of that business, carries out a promotional venture indicating that contributions will be made to or applied for the benefit of a 'charitable institution'.

A charitable institution is a charity or another institution established for charitable, benevolent or philanthropic purposes. Relevant ventures are advertising or sales campaigns and any other venture undertaken for a promotional purpose.

It should be noted that 'solicit' has a very wide meaning in this context. It covers express and implied requests whether they are made by:

- speaking directly to the person or persons to whom the solicitation is addressed;
- a statement published in any newspaper, film, or radio or television programme; or
- other means of communicating.

Anyone responsible for receiving money or property solicited on behalf of a charitable institution is subject to the controls, even if that person did not themselves make the solicitation. For example, if a third party is dealing with the receipts from an appeal made directly by the charity, that third party must comply with the regulatory requirements.

The statutory provisions:

- make it unlawful to solicit money and property on behalf of a charitable institution unless the relevant requirements have been met;
- require a written agreement between the charity and the regulated person (which must address particular matters);
- oblige the fundraiser to make specific statements to the public when making the solicitation; and
- impose criminal sanctions for non-compliance on the fundraiser (rather than the charity).

The precise information required in the statement to the public varies, depending on how the solicitation is made, whether the regulated fundraiser is a professional fundraiser or a commercial participator and whether more than one charitable institution is to benefit from the fundraising activities. Recent reforms have enhanced and clarified the detailed requirements.

Fundraising regulations: Scotland

Fundraising on behalf of charities or other 'benevolent bodies' in Scotland is subject to the requirements of Scottish charity law (see sections 79–83 of the Charities and Trustee Investment (Scotland) Act 2005 and the Charities and Benevolent Fundraising (Scotland) Regulations 2009).

These requirements extend to benevolent fundraisers, professional fundraisers and commercial participators. Further regulations will be made in due course in relation to public collections of cash and goods.

Note that the regulations do not only apply to fundraising for charities on the Scottish Charity Register. Fundraising for any charity or for any 'benevolent body' is affected (i.e. a body set up for benevolent or philanthropic purposes).

A professional fundraiser is a person who carries on a fundraising business or who, in return for a financial reward, seeks money or other property for a benevolent body or for general charitable, benevolent or philanthropic purposes.

A commercial participator is an organisation carrying on a business, other than a fundraising business, that, in the course of the business, takes part in a promotional venture where some or all of the proceeds are to be given to benevolent bodies or used for charitable, benevolent or philanthropic purposes.

A benevolent fundraiser includes benevolent bodies and companies, and extends to individuals:

- in management or control;
- acting as employees or agents; or
- in some situations, acting as a volunteer.

Where the fundraising is undertaken by a professional fundraiser or a commercial participator, a written agreement addressing particular required areas must be entered into between that organisation and the charity.

There are detailed requirements about statements that must be made to the public in such fundraising initiatives, donor cancellation rights and other rules, such as recordkeeping requirements and obligations regarding a transfer of funds from the fundraiser to the beneficiary charity or other benevolent body.

The precise information that must be given to a potential donor varies, depending on whether the solicitation is oral or written and made by a benevolent fundraiser, a professional fundraiser or a commercial participator. It will include information about the intended beneficiary organisation(s) and the remuneration of the fundraiser.

Breaches of the legal requirements lead to criminal offences. Generally the fundraiser will be liable, not the charity.

There are some valuable protections for charities, including rights to challenge and obtain prohibitions on unauthorised fundraising. Initially this can be done by written request but, if that fails, application to the courts will be required.

Charity sector fundraising 'self-regulation'

Some types of fundraising and fundraising relationships are subject to statutory controls and specific regulatory regimes. However, the overall regulation of charity fundraising remains largely dependent on good practice and the so-called 'self-regulatory regime' for charity sector fundraising.

The Institute of Fundraising is the representative body for the charity fundraising community, including individuals who are professional charity fundraisers and commercial fundraising organisations, in particular fundraising charities. The old Public Fundraising Regulatory Association merged with the Institute in August 2016.

Charity fundraisers (including fundraising consultants) are encouraged (but not required by law) to join the Institute, observe its professional standards and enhance their skills and knowledge through its professional development activities. (See www.institute-of-fundraising.org.uk.)

The Fundraising Regulator was established in 2016 as a direct result of recommendations made in the review report 'Regulating Fundraising for the Future' (September 2015). Its set-up costs have been met voluntarily by a number of the largest charities. Its ongoing running costs will be met by a levy paid voluntarily by charities wishing to opt into this new voluntary regime for regulating charity fundraising activities and standards (a sliding scale of levy fees will apply, determined by financial thresholds).

Despite its name, the Regulator is not established by statute (rather it is a 'not-for-profit' non-charitable company limited by guarantee) and it does not have a statutory remit or direct statutory enforcement powers. Instead, it operates a regulatory regime for charity fundraising that is based on a voluntary 'opt-in' system, supported by weighty moral pressure on charities that engage in public fundraising to any significant degree. The Charity Commission expects such charities to join the Fundraising Regulator's scheme but does not currently have power to force them to do so. Increasingly, the Commission and other relevant bodies are likely to encourage other charities that have smaller scale public fundraising activities, to join the Fundraising Regulator's regulatory scheme.

The principal areas of activity for the Fundraising Regulator are:

- Setting and promoting standards of fundraising practice. To this end, the Fundraising Regulator is responsible for updating the Code of Fundraising Practice and for monitoring compliance with the Code.
- Adjudicating complaints received from the public about fundraising practice.
- Investigating cases where fundraising practice has led to significant public concern.
- Operating a 'Fundraising Preference Service'; that enables individuals to make choices about the way charities interact with them regarding fundraising (including 'opt-out' options). At the date of preparation of this edition, the full details of the FPS and its practical operation (including interaction with existing schemes such as the Telephone Preference Service) are still awaited.

The Fundraising Regulator is likely to refer appropriate concerns on to other regulators, such as the Charity Commission, for investigation and possible sanctions. The Commission will take a serious view of any charity that incurs criticism from the regulator and may decide to 'name and shame' in some way. The Commission is also very likely to act on any specific concerns regarding individual charities that the regulator may refer to the Commission.

The Fundraising Regulator itself is not expected to impose direct financial penalties on any organisations or individuals that the regulator considers to have acted in breach of its scheme and relevant Codes and rules.

The Code of Fundraising Practice, the Street Fundraising Rulebook and the Door to Door Fundraising Rulebook can all be accessed on and downloaded from the Fundraising Regulator's website, which also provides other useful guidance, resources and links (see www.fundraisingregulator.org.uk).

Trading

The myth that charities cannot trade is still surprisingly widely believed. In fact charities can trade, both in direct pursuit of their own charitable purposes (often called 'primary purpose trading') and to raise funds, subject to some fundamental conditions:

- They must remain true to their charitable purposes.
- They must not allow the charity or its charitable funds and assets to be used for private gain by individuals (especially trustees or people and organisations connected to trustees) or for substantial commercial gain by third parties.
- They must observe any conditions or restrictions on commercial trading, or investment in commercial companies, that are set out in their constitutions.
- Fundraising trading may only be carried out to a relatively modest level within the charity.

Trustees must make careful judgements about what types of trading may be both possible and appropriate. They should also consider the best structure for trading activities. Larger-scale fundraising trading will need to be carried out through a trading subsidiary.

Trading is a complex and potentially high-risk area for charities. Appropriate professional advice should be taken especially in relation to legal, regulatory and tax aspects.

Trustees' responsibilities

The board of trustees has overall responsibility for all the trading activities carried out by or for the charity. They must consider how any trading activities fit into the charity's overall strategy, ensure the charity operates within its own constitution and address risk management, including reputational risks as well as financial risks.

Trading should be actively managed, with clear objectives and regular monitoring of performance against those objectives. In addition, a broader annual review of the charity's overall trading activities is good practice.

It is important to ensure trading is carried out correctly, as there are personal liability risks for trustees if a charity trades *ultra vires* (beyond its powers) or otherwise unlawfully.

Self-generation of income from direct charitable activities (primary purpose trading)

Charities have always generated income from their own charitable activities, trading in direct pursuit of their charitable purposes with the aim of delivering charitable public benefit – think of a charitable theatre selling tickets to performances, a charitable art gallery charging for admission to a special exhibition or an educational charity selling teaching resources and professional development courses for teachers. Often the charity's beneficiaries are directly engaged in such trading – for example, ex-offenders undertaking window cleaning or gardening work for members of the public, through a charity dedicated to reintegrating ex-offenders into society.

Changes in charity sector funding, new approaches to the delivery of public services and the care of major assets for public use, together with major worldwide economic challenges, have helped add impetus to the self-generation of funds from such 'primary purpose trading'. The UK charity sector generates around 37% of its total income from such trading.

Fundraising trading (non-prim'

Other forms of trading by ch
funds (i.e. the aim is fundra'
benefits). This is known a'

It is important to rec'
trading, is not of itself
(regardless of the fac'
charitable activities'
charitable purpose.

A certain level of fundrais'
directly by the charity (tax free). It '
the detriment of the charity's direct charita'
the charity's charitable status. Larger-scale trading.
threshold and higher-risk trading activities need to be a'
a trading subsidiary.

Social enterprise

Increasingly, some charities use the term 'social enterprise' to describe
their trading activities. Although the term does not have a strict legal
meaning, broadly 'social enterprise' is the carrying out of trading activities for a wider social purpose. The prime objective is to provide social
benefit while also generating some level of surplus funds. Most of those
profits will be reinvested in the activities, though some may be transferred
over to relevant community purposes.

A charity engaging in social enterprise is subject to all the usual
restraints on trading activities. It must ensure the benefits provided to the
wider community by the activities are appropriate to its charitable
purposes. Any gifts of funds generated by the activity must also be made
within its charitable purposes and within the limits of the charity's constitutional powers.

Some social enterprise activities are carried out in a more commercial
setting, with external investors who receive a certain proportion of the
profits from the activities. This would not be appropriate in a charity.

Trading subsidiaries

A trading subsidiary is a commercial company, normally limited by
shares, that is owned and operated by a charity to raise funds. Activities

operly carry out itself (because of its charitable
tial or higher-risk commercial trading activities
hrough a trading subsidiary.

o structure the company as a wholly owned
ion, the subsidiary's articles of association need to
t protections for the charity, such as the right to appoint
e board of directors. Some but not all of the trustees should
ctors, together with some independent directors experienced
ant commercial activities. This helps maintain independent
ce for both entities and also assists in managing potential
ts of interest.

nds invested by the charity in its subsidiary are an investment and
oject to the normal legal rules and principles regarding investments.
Trustees must actively manage the charity's interests in its subsidiary,
setting key objectives and performance criteria, and monitoring the
subsidiary's performance against those. Regular financial reporting to
the trustee board is essential.

Trustees must be careful to avoid risk of loss of charitable funds
invested in a subsidiary. The charity should ensure it obtains security for
any loan it may make to the subsidiary and the loan must be properly
authorised by the trustee board and adequately documented. Care must
be taken to ensure that the subsidiary remains solvent and loss-making
trading should never be subsidised by charitable funds.

A subsidiary is subject to the normal corporate taxation regime, so it
must pay corporation tax on its retained profits. Surplus profits, that are
not required to be retained for the ongoing needs of the business, may be
donated to the parent charity annually, under the Gift Aid scheme. Such a
donation is tax free, as the funds are donated before deduction of tax and
the company can offset the donation sum against its corporation tax
liability for the relevant tax year. Provided the subsidiary is wholly owned
by one or more charities, there is a nine-month time limit, from the end of
the financial year, during which this donation may be made.

Charity shops

Traditional charity shops sell second-hand goods donated to the charity
by its supporters. This amounts to the cash conversion of the donor's gift
and HMRC will not seek to tax the funds generated. The charity can

operate this kind of traditional charity shop activity directly itself, without prejudicing its charitable status, as the activities are not commercial trading activities.

The position is more complex when new goods are being bought in for resale, as that is commercial trading and there may also be tax and VAT issues. Likewise, if the charity wants to operate a scheme to generate Gift Aid through the sale of goods provided by supporters, there are potential legal and tax complications, and the activity must be correctly structured and operated to avoid potentially significant problems. The supporters are not strictly making a genuine gift of the goods. Rather they are providing them for the charity to sell as their agent, then making a separate donation of the amount raised, using Gift Aid. Professional advice should be taken before embarking on these kinds of activities.

Investment

The term 'investment' has a very wide meaning in relation to charitable funds. In its broadest sense it can cover financial investments, made with the intention of growing capital or generating income (or a mix of both), and also investments made with a view to achieving charitable outcomes (sometimes called 'programme-related' or 'social impact' investments).

When considering charity investments, it is important to address:
- what powers the charity has to make investments;*
- what powers the trustees have to make investment decisions;*
- trustees' investment duties;*
- relevant provisions in the charity's constitution (this is particularly important for unincorporated charities); and
- the objectives in making investments – is it financial return (generation of spendable income), capital growth (building the charity's investable capital levels for the future), charitable outcomes or a mixture of these objectives?

* These depend, in part, on the legal form of the charity.

Unincorporated charities

Unincorporated charities have statutory general financial investment powers under the Trustee Act 2000 and a further statutory power to invest in land. These are subject to some limitations and the individual charity's constitution may impose further restrictions. Incorporated charities, in particular charitable companies, usually have implied and uninhibited investment powers (subject to the general constraints of charitable status).

In relation to financial investments, the trustees of unincorporated charities must:

- adopt an investment policy, measure performance of the charity's investments against that policy and report on these matters in their Trustees' Annual Report;
- observe their general statutory duty to exercise reasonable skill and care in relation to investment matters;
- obtain and consider proper independent advice before using their investment powers (it is sensible to keep records of both the advice and the trustees' consideration of it); and
- have regard to the Standard Investment Criteria.

The Standard Investment Criteria are:

- The suitability to the charity of the type of investment being considered.
- The suitability of the particular investment as an investment of that type.
- The need for diversification of the charity's investments, as appropriate to the charity's circumstances.

Charitable companies

For charitable companies, the specific legal rules in the Trustee Act are not compulsory. However, their trustees are subject to the usual general duties of trustees and it is good practice to adopt an investment policy with clear objectives and to measure actual investment performance. There should also be transparent public reporting.

Scottish charities

For Scottish charities, the statutory investment rules in the Charities and Trustee Investment (Scotland) Act 2005 apply (whatever the legal form of the charity and regardless of whether or not that is an incorporated legal form). These provide a statutory investment power and impose duties on the trustees to obtain and consider proper advice about the way in which the investment power should be used and, also, to have regard to:

- the suitability to the charity of the proposed investment; and
- the need for diversification of the charity's investments, as appropriate to its circumstances.

Social investment

Social investment (sometimes called 'social impact investment') is investment made partly with the aim of a financial return and also with the intention of a social return – an expectation of a positive social impact from the activities that are being funded. That impact is an inherent part of the overall intended outcomes and benefits.

Trustees must ensure that social investment of charitable funds is only undertaken within the charity's charitable purposes and within its powers. Any restrictions in the charity's constitution must be observed and the usual risk assessments made. Subsequently, the trustees should monitor the actual performance against the investment objectives, both with regard to the financial returns and the charitable impact.

Social Investments – Charities (Protection and Social Investment) Act 2016

This Act provides a statutory power for most (but not all) charities to make social investments. The provisions are intended to clarify the legal position in order to encourage and facilitate social investment of charitable funds.

This statutory power is not available to charities that are Royal Charter bodies or statutory charities.

In addition, generally the power cannot be used to make social investments with endowment funds.

Other potential restrictions might arise because of the provisions of the particular charity's constitution.

The Act specifies that the relevant charities may invest with a view to both:

- Directly furthering the charity's purposes; and
- Achieving a financial return for the charity.

In deciding whether or not to exercise this power, the trustees have specific duties to:

- consider whether they should obtain advice;
- consider any advice that they do obtain; and

- consider whether it is in the best interests of the charity's charitable purposes to invest:
  - In direct furtherance of those purposes; and
  - to achieve a financial return.

If the charity is unincorporated and thus subject to the Trustee Act 2000, these duties override the Trustee Act Standard Investment Criteria. However, they do not override the trustees' general duty of care under the Trustee Act.

In addition, the trustees of any charity using this power have a further duty to review their charity's social investments from time to time.

All other legal principles and rules of charity law apply to social investments and the exercise of this power, including the restrictions on private benefits and the rules on conflicts of interest.

Tax and VAT

Charities do not have blanket exemption from either direct taxation or from VAT. However, they can benefit from a range of specific charity tax exemptions and reliefs provided they meet the relevant conditions for the particular exemption or relief claimed. Access to these exemptions and reliefs is not automatic; the charity must apply to HMRC for recognition and verify that it meets the tax test of being a charity. The criteria for meeting this test are specified by tax law and are not exactly the same as the criteria for being a charity in charity law. They include the 'management condition', which requires the organisation to ensure all its trustees and senior managers are 'fit and proper persons'.

Guidance on applying for charity tax recognition and on the applicable conditions, including the 'fit and proper persons' test, with the relevant application form, is on HMRC's website: www.hmrc.gov.uk/charities.

A charity's donated income and investment income are not normally subject to tax. Gifts of securities (including shares) and real property (i.e. land and buildings) to a charity are usually tax free, as are gifts made to a charity under a will.

Provided it is applied exclusively to the charity's charitable purposes, income generated from the charity's primary purpose trading (trading in direct pursuit of its charitable purposes) is generally exempt from tax.

Fundraising trading income is not subject to a blanket tax exemption. However, there is a small-scale trading tax exemption for income from a charity's own fundraising trading, provided the funds raised do not exceed 25% of the charity's total incoming resources (up to a maximum level of £50,000 a year) (section 46 of the Finance Act 2000). Modest levels of commercial trading by a charity, such as sales of Christmas cards, can therefore potentially be carried out tax free. This exemption does not apply to trading subsidiaries.

Where a charity occupies and uses premises for its charitable purposes, it is entitled to 80% mandatory rate relief from non-domestic rates (i.e. business rates). The relevant local authority may grant the additional 20% relief on a discretionary basis. Various conditions apply, including a requirement for the premises to be used wholly or mainly for the charity's charitable purposes.

There is no blanket exemption from VAT for charities. However, there is some limited VAT relief available to charities (largely in Schedules 8 and 9 of the VAT Act 1994). These do not apply to trading subsidiaries.

Tax and VAT issues relating to charities can be complex and potentially risky, so suitable professional advice should be obtained.

Appendix 1

Role description for charity trustee

Trustee of [name of charity]:

Charity no:

Company no [if applicable]:

ROLE	To ensure, with the other trustees, that the charity acts in accordance with its constitution and to manage its activities in furtherance of the charitable purposes set out in that constitution.
NOTE	The charity is registered as a charity [and a limited company] [in the form of an unincorporated trust]. Every trustee [is also a director of the company and] has legal responsibilities and potential liabilities in [each] [that] capacity. Full details of these are not included in this role description, but can be obtained from the charity's office.

Responsibilities

- Setting strategy and undertaking the strategic management of the charity.

- Ensuring that the charity complies with its [Articles of Association] [trust deed] [constitution] and all applicable legislation and regulations.

- Ensuring that the charity pursues its charitable purposes for the public benefit (its charitable purposes are set out in its [Articles] [trust deed] [constitution]).

- Ensuring that the charity applies its resources in pursuance of its charitable purposes and provides appropriate public benefit through its activities in pursuit of those purposes.

- Ensuring the financial stability and solvency of the charity.

- Ensuring proper accounting records are kept.

- Ensuring the effective and efficient administration of the charity.

- Protecting and managing the property of the charity.

- Ensuring the proper investment of the charity's funds.

- Approving the charity's policies.

- Safeguarding the good name and ethos of the charity.

Duties

Collective

Example:

- Approving the rolling [five-year] plan annually and monitoring progress against it.
- Determining/approving the annual budget and monitoring progress against it.
- Preparing and approving the annual report and accounts.
- Appointing the Chief Executive and monitoring the post holder's performance.

Individual

Example:

- Attending meetings of trustees.
- Playing an active part in the trustees' meetings and deliberations.
- Exercising due care and attention, and using reasonable skill in dealing with the charity's affairs.
- Using the trustee's own skills, knowledge and experience to help the board of trustees reach sound decisions.
- Taking the lead in any trustees' activities where the trustee has special knowledge.
- Avoiding any conflict of interests and declaring potential conflicts to the board of trustees.
- Sitting on the Finance and General Purposes Committee if required.
- Serving on one or more [committees] [sub-committees] [Advisory Groups].
- Sitting on recruitment and disciplinary panels if required.

Appendix 2

Role description for chairman

Chairman of [name of charity]:

Charity no:

Company no [if applicable]:

ROLE	To lead the charity's board of trustees, ensuring that it fulfils its responsibilities for the governance of the charity; to work in partnership with the Chief Executive to pursue the charity's charitable purposes effectively; and to optimise the relationship between the trustees, the staff and volunteers.

Responsibilities

- Leadership of the board of trustees (as the governing body of the charity) in its role of setting the direction and strategy of the charity.

- Ensuring that the board of trustees acts in furtherance of the charity's charitable purposes.

- Ensuring that the board of trustees deploys the charity's resources to further the charity's charitable purposes for the public benefit and in accordance with legal requirements.

- Planning the annual cycle of board meetings and committee meetings.

- Setting the agenda for meetings of the board of trustees.

- Ensuring that decisions taken at meetings are implemented.

Duties

Example:

- Chairing meetings of the board of trustees and [Finance and General Purposes Committee].

- Liaising regularly with the Chief Executive to maintain an overview of the charity's affairs and to provide support and guidance as appropriate.

- Being an ambassador for the charity.

- Representing the charity when appropriate at functions and meetings.

- Acting as a spokesperson when appropriate.

- Leading the process of appraising the Chief Executive.

- Sitting on appointment panels for senior staff.

- Chairing the pay review group.

- Sitting on disciplinary panels.

NOTES

1. This specimen is intended for use by a charity that has an employed Chief Executive and staff team. Appropriate adjustments should be made if using for a purely volunteer-run charity.

2. Adapt terminology as appropriate (e.g. 'Chief Executive' or 'Chief Executive Officer', 'board of trustees' or 'council of management'). Ensure consistency with the charity's constitution, with staff job descriptions and job titles, etc.

Appendix 3

Role description for treasurer

Treasurer of [name of charity]:

Charity no:

Company no [if applicable]:

ROLE	To maintain an overview of the charity's financial affairs, ensuring that it is financially viable and solvent; to ensure that proper financial procedures are operated and that proper records are kept.

Responsibilities

- Ensuring that the financial resources of the charity meet its present and future needs and obligations.

- Ensuring that the charity has and follows an appropriate policy on financial reserves.

- Ensuring that proper accounting records are kept.

- Ensuring that appropriate accounting procedures and financial controls are in place.

- Advising on the financial implications of the charity's [five-year] plan.

- Ensuring that the charity has and follows an appropriate investment policy.

- Ensuring that there is no conflict between any investment held and the charitable purposes of the charity.

- Ensuring that all legal restrictions on funds, investments and fundraising are complied with.

- Ensuring that the accounts are audited or independently examined in accordance with applicable accounting standards and as required by law (if applicable), and that any recommendations of the auditor or independent examiner are properly addressed.

- Ensuring that the accounts are prepared in the form required by law and the relevant regulations, in particular the Charity Commission and/or the Office of the Scottish Charity Regulator and/or the Charity Commission for Northern Ireland [and the Registrar of Companies].

Duties

Example:

- Overseeing, approving and presenting budgets, accounts and financial statements.
- Preparing and presenting (together with staff) financial reports to the trustees.
- Keeping trustees informed about their financial duties and responsibilities.
- Liaising with staff and volunteers as necessary concerning financial matters.
- Contributing to the setting of the fundraising strategy of the charity.
- Making a formal presentation of the accounts at the annual general meeting, drawing attention to important points in an accessible manner.*
- Sitting on the Finance and General Purposes Committee.
- Sitting on recruitment and disciplinary panels as required.

NOTES

1. If the charity is unincorporated, it is not necessary for the annual accounts to be filed with the Registrar of Companies.

2. If the charity is very small, it may be exempt from filing its annual accounts with the Charity Commission. There are no comparable exemptions for charities on the Scottish Charity Register.

3. This specimen assumes the charity has an employed Chief Executive and staff team. Appropriate adjustments should be made if using for a purely volunteer-run charity.

4. Adapt terminology as appropriate (e.g. 'Chief Executive' or 'Chief Executive Officer', 'board of trustees' or 'council of management'). Ensure consistency with the charity's constitution, with staff job descriptions and job titles, etc.

5. * Delete if the charity does not have a formal membership (e.g. it is an unincorporated charitable trust) or is not obliged to hold AGMs and present its annual accounts at such meetings.

Appendix 4

Role description for secretary of a charitable company

Secretary of [name of charity]:

Charity no:

Company no:

ROLE	To ensure that the conduct of the charity complies with all relevant requirements of charity and company law; and to support the chairman by ensuring the smooth functioning of the board of trustees.

Responsibilities

- Facilitating the good governance of the charity.

- Ensuring that relevant legal requirements are drawn to the attention of trustees and are complied with.

- Ensuring that proper arrangements are made for the calling, conduct and recording of the annual general meeting or other general meetings of the charity's members.

- Ensuring that all matters relating to the admission and cessation of membership of the charity and the appointment or cessation of office of trustees and officers are conducted in accordance with the charity's articles of association.

- Ensuring that proper arrangements are made for the calling, conduct and recording of trustees' meetings.

- Ensuring that statutory registers are kept as required by the Companies Act 2006 and associated regulations.

Duties

Example:

The following duties may be delegated to staff or volunteers in whole or part, but it remains the responsibility of the secretary to ensure that they are carried out:

- Preparing documents for, ensuring the proper conduct of and making records of all general meetings of the members.

- Preparing documents for, ensuring the proper conduct of and making records of all trustees' meetings.

- Ensuring necessary actions are taken in consequence of meetings.

- Ensuring required documents and information are provided to the Registrar of Companies and the Charity Commission, and/or the Office of the Scottish Charity Regulator and/or the Charity Commission for Northern Ireland (as appropriate).

- Ensuring the charity keeps statutory registers in compliance with the Companies Act 2006 and relevant regulations.

NOTE

1. If the company does not hold annual general meetings, remove references to AGMs.

Appendix 5

Role description for secretary of an unincorporated membership charity

Secretary of [name of charity]:

Charity no:

ROLE	To ensure that the conduct of the charity complies with all relevant requirements of charity law; and to support the chairman by ensuring the smooth functioning of the board of trustees.

Responsibilities

- Facilitating the good governance of the charity.

- Ensuring that relevant legal requirements are drawn to the attention of trustees and are complied with.

- Ensuring that proper arrangements are made for the calling, conduct and recording of annual meetings or other formal meetings of the charity's members.

- Ensuring that all matters relating to the admission and cessation of membership of the charity and the appointment or cessation of office of trustees and officers are conducted in accordance with the charity's constitution.

- Ensuring that proper arrangements are made for the calling, conduct and recording of trustees' meetings.

Duties

Example:

The following duties may be delegated to staff or volunteers in whole or part, but it remains the responsibility of the secretary to ensure that they are carried out:

- Preparing documents for, ensuring the proper conduct of and making records of all formal meetings of the members.

- Preparing documents for, ensuring the proper conduct of and making records of all trustees' meetings.

- Ensuring necessary actions are taken in consequence of meetings.

- Ensuring required documents and information are provided to the Charity Commission and/or the Office of the Scottish Charity Regulator and/or Charity Commission for Northern Ireland (as appropriate).

NOTE

1. This specimen can be adapted for a clerk to the trustees of an unincorporated charitable trust (delete references to members and members' meetings in that case).

Web directory

Advisory, Conciliation and Arbitration Service (ACAS)
www.acas.org.uk

Charity Commission
www.charity-commission.gov.uk

Charity Commission for Northern Ireland
www.charitycommissionni.org.uk

Charity Governance Code
www.governancecode.org

Companies House
www.companieshouse.gov.uk

Disclosure and Barring Service
www.gov.uk/government/organisations/disclosure-and-barring-service

Fundraising Regulator
www.fundraisingregulator.org.uk

Health and Safety Executive (HSE)
www.hse.gov.uk

Her Majesty's Revenue & Customs (HMRC)
www.hmrc.gov.uk

Home Office
www.homeoffice.gov.uk

ICSA – The Governance Institute
www.icsa.org.uk

Information Commissioner's Office
www.ico.gov.uk

Institute of Fundraising
www.institute-of-fundraising.org.uk

The Office of the Scottish Charity Regulator (OSCR)
www.oscr.org.uk

Index

670806
0967121S